The Magic Presence

ASCENDED MASTER
DISCOURSES

BY THE ASCENDED MASTERS
THROUGH GODFRE RAY KING

* * *

"I AM" Religious Activity
of the
SAINT GERMAIN FOUNDATION

* * * *

SAINT GERMAIN PRESS, INC.
1120 Stonehedge Drive
Schaumburg, Illinois 60194

Library of Congress Cataloging-in-Publication Data

Ascended master discourses.

(Saint Germain series ; v. 6)

1. I AM Religious Activity. I. King, Godfré Ray, 1878-1939. II. Series.

BP605.I18A8   1986   299'.93   85-1778

ISBN: 1-878891-28-6

"I AM" RELIGIOUS ACTIVITY
of the
SAINT GERMAIN FOUNDATION

The "I AM" Religious Activity represents the Original, Permanent, and Highest Source of the Ascended Masters' Instruction on the Great Laws of Life, as first offered to the Western World by the Ascended Master Saint Germain through His Accredited Messengers, Mr. and Mrs. Guy W. Ballard.

In the early 1930's the Ballards established the Saint Germain Foundation and Saint Germain Press, Inc., which under Saint Germain's Guidance have expanded into worldwide organizations that offer to mankind the True Ascended Master Teachings on the Great Cosmic Words, "I AM"! The Saint Germain Foundation strives to keep this "I AM" Ascended Master Instruction in Its pure, unadulterated form, free from any human interpretation, personal monetary gain, or any proselytizing, as It is a Gift from the Great Ascended Masters and Cosmic Beings to bring Illumination and Perfection to mankind.

Hundreds of "I AM" Sanctuaries and "I AM" Temples exist throughout the world, where the Teachings are applied in "I AM" Decree Groups. The Books of the Saint Germain Series are available through the Saint Germain Press, Inc. and in many libraries and bookstores. For further information please contact:

SAINT GERMAIN FOUNDATION
SAINT GERMAIN PRESS, INC.
1120 Stonehedge Drive
Schaumburg, Illinois 60194
(708) 882-7400
(800) 662-2800

THE SAINT GERMAIN SERIES

DEDICATION

HIS series of Books is dedicated in deepest
Eternal Love and Gratitude to our Beloved
Ascended Masters, Saint Germain, Jesus,
Nada, the Great Divine Director, the Great White
Brotherhood, the Brotherhood of the Royal Teton,
the Brotherhood of Mount Shasta, the Great Ones
from Venus, and those other Ascended Masters
whose loving Help has been direct and without limit.

TRIBUTE

N THIS hour of world crisis, the Great Ascended Masters are giving every Assistance possible to the "I AM" Students and all who sincerely seek the Light throughout America and the world. This takes place through Their Projection of Light Rays which are an Outpouring of Light-Substance from the Ascended Masters' Octave of Life.

The various Ascended Masters who dictated these Discourses have each one given Their own Radiance in and through the Words themselves. It does not matter who doubts this Great Truth, Law, and Activity; the Great Ascended Masters and these Dictations are the Mightiest Law, Reality, and Blessing that have ever come to mankind in hundreds of years. They come as a glad free Gift of Love and contain only Perfection for all. They radiate the Feeling to the Student and reader that he too may become Master of himself and his world and rise into the Full Freedom and Victory of the Ascension.

Each Book is sent forth as a Blazing Golden Sun, charged with the Ascended Masters' Consciousness, Substance, Love, Light, Wisdom, and Perfection — with the Power of a Thousand Suns — to illumine, set free, protect, supply, bless, and produce Perfection for all who read or contact them.

TRIBUTE

Through these Books all shall feel the Mighty Truth and Activity of these Great Ones, to the fullness of the Freedom and the Ascension of all mankind.

GODFRE RAY KING

FOREWORD

HIS Book is given to the "I AM" Students and readers to help them feel the Closeness and Reality of the Blessed Ascended Masters. Through this feeling these Great Ones will be able to pour forth a Mighty Radiance of Light and Love from Their Octave of Life. In this way Ascended Master Assistance can be given to all who will feel the Reality of these Mighty Beings deeply; for that feeling will enable the Student or reader to reach up and make conscious effort and Application for his own Eternal Freedom—the Ascension.

The Discourses contained herein were dictated in Words of Living Light to me before thousands of "I AM" Students, who felt the Closeness and Reality of the Ascended Masters unmistakably—in their own physical bodies and the atmosphere of the room. They are given to the public in the same phraseology as the Students heard them, for they were conversations to help the Students solve their problems and gain Self-control in their efforts toward Mastery. These Marvelous Discourses will convey the same feeling and activity to all who read them, if the reader will place himself in the position of the Students and feel the Masters are speaking to him direct, because all mankind's problems are similar and all need the same explanation to give them Mastery over themselves, which means obedience of their human feelings and attention to the Great Law of Life—the "Mighty I AM Presence."

Each Book is charged with the Light, Love, Substance, Energy, and Vibration from the Ascended Masters' own Octave of Life and from Their Ascended Bodies, to step up the vibratory action of those who read or contact them, and through that, to release Ascended Master Qualities into all the physical experiences of the individual.

The action of this is the same as that of our physical Sun upon the plant life of our world. By Radiation from above, the fullness of the Divine Plan is expanded into the physical manifestation of this world, and the individual himself becomes an Ascended Master through obedience to the Law of Life, the "Mighty I AM Presence."

GODFRE RAY KING

CONTENTS

ASCENDED MASTER
DISCOURSES

By THE ASCENDED MASTERS

SAINT GERMAIN'S DISCOURSE

SHRINE AUDITORIUM CLASS — LOS ANGELES, CALIFORNIA

JANUARY 1, 1937

BELOVED Ones, there are a few announcements I wish to make before I begin My talk to you. It seems pitiful that We should again have to mention this: one whom We have trusted is being tempted to go forth saying he is receiving the Light and Sound Ray from Jesus, when he is not. Unless this thing ceases among the Students, it will be Our unhappy duty to report him by name. Now let this cease forever. When such a thing comes forth, it will be unmistakable and We will know it.

As long as these Beloved Messengers go forth in this Work, We shall not project any Tangible, Visible Tube of Light to anyone — and all the Ascended Masters are One. This Work must be kept clean and pure, and We shall see that It is.

During this Class, I have not had an opportunity to

1

announce My Request to the Messengers, but they will
have a month free for broadcasting, if they so wish.
Then there will be a Class in San Francisco and in
Dallas, Texas. The announcement of the dates will
be made as soon as the Messengers have time to make
the arrangements.

I want you Precious Children of the Light, if you
will, to realize that We are Real, Tangible Beings.
We know everything that is going on in your mind,
motive, and intent; and We are standing guard over
this Work, make no mistake about it! You might
deceive the Messengers, but you will never deceive Us,
not one.

I tell you, Dear Hearts, with such a Transcendent
Privilege before you, how can anyone allow the claw
of the sinister force to seize upon him and make him
attempt to do unkind and mistaken things? Now,
Beloved Ones, stand guard over yourselves and your
worlds, with all the Power of your "Mighty I AM
Presence." I tell you, when Students or other individuals become so unenlightened that they can
criticize our Beloved Messengers, they are making a
great mistake.

I tell you, Beloved Ones, Law is Law, and We
know the Law in spite of any human opinion to the
contrary! If you will not believe the Law after all the
Infinite Proof which stands before you, then We can
not help you; but remember there is no human being

so important in this World that there are not plenty ready to take his place.

You must understand that I am speaking with all the Love of My Being in sending forth these Words, but I am firm and determined. Our Beloved Messengers, the beloved Sindelars, and the beloved Rogers have battled down walls of human creation. They are not going to have to do it any longer. If there are any battles on, We will take a hand. Now Dear Ones, this is in all kindness; do not go out and accuse Me of being a fighting Ascended Master, but I mean business! These Beloved Messengers, without a word of complaining, have battled down human walls that have been set up against them. They have won their Eternal Victory. I bless them forever for the strength and courage which I said was in them in the beginning, and it has been proved true.

Therefore, Dear Hearts, I speak in this manner to you in the beginning of this New Year, that you may have the full power and conviction of My Words active within you, which stand guard with you and for you and your Eternal Protection.

Those who will not control themselves and shut out the human discord, criticism, condemnation, jealousy, or whatever the activity may be, cannot have Our Help, I tell you. We have pled and pled and pled with the Students all over America and said that self-control was the important thing to be maintained for their

Freedom. Dear Beloved, Precious Ones, if you will not listen to Us who know the Law—having gone the way, every step of it you have to go, and in far more severe conditions than you have today—then We cannot help you.

This Work will go on—do not worry about that! But if you will allow Us, We want to protect you, We want to help you; but We cannot help you if you are going to continue in this kind of thing. When the Beloved Messengers leave the cities in some places and I see disturbance comes in, how can the beloved Students permit it? One human being wants to govern another and set up laws—when the Laws are in the Books! The Group Outline, the Divine Director has sanctioned and asked to be used. Some unhappy individuals have accused Mr. Rogers of having brought out that Group Leaders' regulation. Every word of it is from the Books or Magazines. He simply brought it together, and it was blessed and sanctioned by the Divine Director.

Beloved Ones who are visiting Students and Group Leaders from the different parts of the United States, please carry this word from Me: Any Group Leader who does not wish to follow that Outline, please do not be a Group Leader! We wish to bring a regulated activity which will be a Mighty Focus throughout the United States, for the Freedom and Blessing of mankind and for its protection. If We cannot be obeyed when We know and, through the kindness of the Law, bring before you that which will enable you to be free, then again We cannot help you. It is so imperative at this time! Tremendous protection has been given the coast of America. Do you want to undo this, Beloved Students everywhere, and let this cataclysm come forth and destroy you all, just because you will not control your human impulses?

Precious Ones everywhere, awaken! Oh, awaken to the importance of this! You have become one with this Mighty Stream of Light. Why will you not protect It instead of criticizing It? I am not speaking to the precious ones who have not criticized, you know that; but I am speaking everywhere to those in the mental and feeling world who have done this.

Precious Ones, let us come in as one Great Pillar of Light in the future, and make this year one of the most magnificent in the Victory of the "Mighty I AM Presence" which has ever been known in the history of the World. It can be and it will be done! Will you join It or step aside?

Oh, that you could for one moment know the Great Love that We have poured forth to you—the whole entire Group of Ascended Masters. The Messengers have poured out Love and called It forth from the "Mighty I AM Presence" without limit. You have poured forth so great a Love. I am speaking to a few who have been critical: oh, Beloved, Precious

Ones, take command of the human self and silence its activity forever. It is only yourselves whom you injure, Precious Ones. After all that has been said by the Messengers, how can you fail to comprehend that every discordant thing you send out is but injuring yourselves? You cannot harm this Work nor the Messengers; but you do harm yourselves, sometimes irreparably.

Our Love is so great for you, and I say again as I did in the East, I have the confidence that My Love is great enough to redeem everyone. One day when they see the missed opportunity, the Hearts of those who have temporarily stepped aside will cry out for the Radiance which they have left.

Precious Ones, oh, that you could understand and feel the great, great Love which enfolds you. Our Beloved Nada during this Class has performed one of the most Transcendent Services for every one of you, enfolding you in Her Infinite Substance of Divine Love. Our Precious Nada—there has been very little said about Her, but I am going to say something tonight which you will never forget: In civilization after civilization She has been the Inspiration and the Power to lift them to the height! Such is the privilege you have in receiving the Radiance of Our Beloved Nada, who made the Ascension before Jesus.

Do you still feel, oh, My Precious Ones, that these

Great Beings are just an imagination of the Messengers? Is it possible that such still can be the case? I trust not. The Service rendered to humanity is inconceivable to one in the limitations of the flesh. Still, you Blessed, Precious Ones who have been drawn under this Radiance by My Humble Efforts, have serving you these Marvelous Beings, Transcendent beyond all concept of the average individual. Oh, every Precious One, awaken and let your Heart release Its Feeling and Understanding of these Mighty Truths for you!

Now then, We shall pass this matter by, and in behalf of Jesus, Beloved Nada, and the Beloved Divine Director, I extend Their and My Gratitude, Thanks, and Congratulations to the beloved Students, to the many who were able to reach the Royal Teton last night. Ten thousand two hundred and twenty-seven were there last evening. It was a wonderful thing, and a Service was rendered heretofore unknown in the history of the Earth. This Service will continue for the first seven days of the New Year from all of the Retreats: the one north of Suva; the one in Arabia; Chananda's Home—the Cave of Light in India; the Cave of Symbols; the Royal Teton, and the various Temples of Light.

As the Beloved Messenger Mrs. Ballard has said, the Earth is being drenched by these Great Rays of Light and Energy. Every Effort is being made to give

Protection, Blessing, and Freedom to the Earth. Why? My Precious Ones, because of your great love poured forth and that of the Students throughout the United States. This Call has enabled things to be done which were impossible without it. Make no mistake about it — your eastern coast and your California coast would have disappeared if this had not been done. Now let the arrogance of the human mind deny that, if it will!

Dear Ones, how willing the human is to have opinions; but remember those never change the Law of Life. I will later give the Messengers the full detail of the marvelous Activity at the Royal Teton last night, so you all may have it.

Within you, oh, Beloved Ones, has been a transcendent activity during the past year — one which should be infinitely encouraging to all of you, and I am sure it is. Oh, the great volume of your love that has poured forth! How We rejoiced and endeavored in Our humble way to convey back to you Our Love, Strength, and Courage.

Beloved Ones, your "Mighty I AM Presence" is your Infinite health, your Infinite strength, your Infinite peace, happiness, and courage, just waiting for you to be harmonious enough so Its Great, Its Mighty Energy can pour forth unqualified by any discordant feeling. Do not expect the Energy from the Great "Presence" to give you relief if you refuse to harmonize yourself enough to stop qualifying that wonderful Energy as you call it forth. Do you not see, Precious Ones, how simple it is and yet so majestic in its action?

Many, many call forth this Mighty Energy with great earnestness and in an unguarded moment requalify it, then wonder why they are distressed. Oh, Precious Ones, will you for your own sake, every time something discordant occurs, stop! still yourselves! and say: "Now what did I do which caused that? 'Mighty I AM Presence,' take it out of me! Annihilate the cause and effect of whatever did it! If it is some past accumulation, 'Mighty I AM Presence,' keep me reminded to call You into action to use the Violet Consuming Flame to consume everything of the past, so something destructive cannot rush forth into outer activity." It is because you do not do this, that you get into difficulty.

I want to call your attention to another activity also: Dear Ones, sometimes part of a family accepts this Great and Wonderful Knowledge and some of them do not. Sometimes their criticism and disturbance brings them into disaster. Oh, it seems so strange that all will not see the Great Law which is acting all the time within you, Dear Hearts. Do you not see that you become the Great Law of your world through your visualization, your feeling, and your qualification? This Mighty Stream of Energy from your "Presence" is constantly flowing through you, filled with Love, Kindness, and Perfection; and you still keep requalifying It with discordant feelings—compelling It to take on the wrong qualities. Then that discord spreads into your world. It cannot help it! It is not the fault of your "Presence," but your uncontrolled human keeps doing that and keeps you in distress.

Tonight while I am talking to you in this Heart-to-Heart manner, a Great Work is going on. We try to help by strengthening you all with that which you require to become master of your feeling, to enable you to govern it, to cause it to come into harmonious obedience to the Great "Presence." Its Great Stream of Energy is intensifying each day, pouring forth through you, trying to bless and carry Perfection into your world.

Oh, My Loved Ones, try now to feel this so earnestly, so vividly active within you that never again will anyone be tempted to feel unkind or give expression to discord. You could be so quickly free if you would only do this. We cannot compel you, Precious Ones; but We plead and plead with such earnestness for you to understand so you do call the "Presence" into action to govern it.

Oh, We love you so greatly. We know what your struggles are, even better than you do, because We have gone through all of them. In My early experience you might be interested to know, Precious Ones, that sometimes things were so terrifying, My hair fairly stood on end, in the experiences I had to go through to gain the Victory!

Today you have the Infinite Assistance of the Cosmic Law and the Great Ascended Ones, which We did not have in Our day of Victory. I call this to your attention for your strength and courage, that you may rise in the Strength of your "Mighty I AM Presence" and win your Victory quickly. It is so easy now, and the Love is so great which is being poured out to you from everywhere — not only the Great Love of the Messengers, but from the Students everywhere as these Classes are held all over the United States. Their great Love is pouring out to you from their "Mighty I AM Presence" like a mighty river, and the numerous telegrams are proof of it. Individuals would not go to the expense of sending telegrams if they were not sincere in their feelings. So, Dear Ones, please awaken! Realize that such is the opportunity before you, for your great Freedom, Glory, Attainment, Victory, and Ascension.

Today, when the Beloved Master Jesus spoke to you, what do you think was going on? The Call had been made by all of you here, that His Ascended Master Consciousness of the Ascension be anchored within your feeling world — and It was this afternoon! Do you not see how, Precious Ones, your Calls are constantly being answered?

In the fullness of this Great Light, the Infinite "Mighty I AM Presence," We call It forth to clothe you in Its Invincible Protection, in Its All-powerful Self-control, in Its All-powerful Joy and Happiness to enfold you this hour—that you may carry it throughout the New Year unto your Victory and even the Ascension.

May I remind you again that when you call forth your "Presence," anything—even the Ascension—is possible for you to attain. Who shall say in the outer world what is the Power of your "Presence" to act in a given moment, when your human has receded enough? This is the Truth which is before you. You have made earnest Calls for many months. Do you think that can go on without having gained a powerful momentum? Then today who shall say—I repeat it again—what your "Presence" can do for you on a moment's notice? In a moment when great Joy, Serenity, and Harmony fill your being, who shall say what your "Mighty I AM Presence" will do for you? Do not limit It, I plead with you. Feel always: any moment, your "Mighty I AM Presence" may sweep into action and perform the most Wonderful Service for you. This is true. It can do it! I cannot say to you *when* It shall; but I do say to you with all Power, all Truth, that your "Presence" is not limited in any sense when your earnest, sincere Call has gone forth, if you will keep your feelings harmonized and keep using the

Violet Consuming Flame so all past accumulations are kept dissolved within your Tube of Light.

Behold that Chart! See that Tube of Light which is really about every one of you. If you keep discord dissolved within that Tube of Light, by the use of the Violet Consuming Flame to annihilate all past discord and creations, then who shall say what moment your "Presence" will sweep into action—as It did with this Good Brother—and render a Service Transcendent beyond description? I want you to feel this, to know it is every bit true and that it is possible for every one of you! There is no limitation to the Action of your "Presence."

Oh, Beloved Ones, the Glory that fills this room tonight ought almost to lift all now into their Ascension by Its Great Love, Its Great Light, Its Great Substance, Its Great Power. Precious Ones, will you feel that everything We try to do and to which We call your attention, is for obedience, help, and assistance, and is always done with the kindest Love in the world. It is because We love you so much that We offer correction through which you may be free.

I want you to just realize, oh, Precious Ones, this Beloved Messenger has been willing to write by the hour [autographing books] to convey My Radiance to you for your Assistance. Tonight he wrote for two hours without cessation. Again I marvel at what these Beloved Ones are able to do—how they are able to govern the flesh to do these things—all for their love of you! Oh, how deep their gratitude is for your love to them. We see all that. We do not just only feel It, We see Its action in and for them. It is beautiful, It is wonderful, It is magnificent, oh, Precious Ones.

Tonight let us feel the Glory of God, the "Mighty I AM Presence," in full action within each one of you—glorifying, purifying, dissolving, and cleansing all past accumulation of whatever discord there has been. Great Infinite "I AM Presence"! at the Call of these loved ones, by the use of Your Violet Consuming Flame, consume all discord now and set these loved ones free. "Mighty I AM Presence" of these blessed ones who are gathered here! Seize all discordantly qualified energy of these beloved ones, of the past and present! Dissolve and consume it in Thy Violet Consuming Flame! Set these loved ones free now! When they go forth at the close of this Class, send them forth free—wholly free—from every discordant activity in the World. Clothe them with Thy Great Feeling of Courage, Strength, Happiness, and Energy. See that they never lack for any of it. Then with Thy Great Commanding, Directing Intelligence, sweep them forward into the Victory and Glory of God, the Mighty "Light of God that never fails." This is Our Love and Wish for you for the New Year.

Eternal Light, Eternal Love, Eternal Mastery! Enter into the feeling world now of every one of these loved ones. God, the "Mighty I AM Presence," through their feeling give them full Mastery and Dominion. Send them forth Thy Mighty Blazing Suns of Light, to pour forth such a Radiance everywhere they move that people are healed, blessed, prospered, and enlightened everywhere their Radiance goes.

O "Mighty I AM Presence" and Great Host of Ascended Masters, glorify the "I AM" Students everywhere they move with such great Love, Peace, Harmony, and Kindliness that people will turn to look at them in wonder. Such is the privilege of the "I AM" Students throughout the World.

"Mighty I AM Presence," guard these Children of Light and give Us the opportunity to give all Assistance that We love to give — to bless, to prosper and set them free. Glorify them now!

The Blessings of the combined Ascended Host be upon our two Beloved Ones [Don and Marjory]. May your path be one of happiness and the "Light of God" victorious everywhere.

I extend to you all and the Students everywhere throughout the United States and the World, the combined Love and Assistance of the Great Host of Ascended Masters, the Legion of Light, and the Angels of Blue Lightning, to act with full Power throughout this year for your happiness, comfort, prosperity, and blessing. Try to accept this in the fullness of your feeling, and let the Mighty Law operate in your world.

In the fullness of My Heart, I love you, I love you, I love you, unto your Ascension; and may that Love lift you quickly into your Freedom and Ascension.

THE GOD MERU'S DISCOURSE

ROGERS' 100% GROUP — LOS ANGELES, CALIFORNIA

JANUARY 21, 1937

MY CHILDREN of the Light, in your song tonight acknowledging the Freedom of America, you brought the release of a Great Cosmic Power. As My Focus of Activity is in South America, so do I join in the Freedom of the Americas and the World.

Children of the Light, be forever certain and reminded by the Great Host of Ascended Masters, of the majestic privileges you have in rendering a Service to the great mass, unknown in the history of mankind. A few have had this privilege, but you today are Children of the Light from many civilizations in which you have lived—sometimes higher, sometimes not so high. Yet in this embodiment, you enter into the culmination, the balancing of that which your Inner Light has sought in every embodiment.

Tonight there is one in your city from South America whom I have been watching for some time. As you may have observed, We never lose an opportunity to watch the Expansion of the Light in every one of the beloved Children of the Light, until their Light expands to the point where We may give

17

Assistance to quicken It into the fullness of Its Mighty Glory—that the individual may become a Blazing Sun of Light wherever he moves, and that We may envelop such a one and pour forth a Mighty Radiance.

Precious Ones of the Light, oh, that you might fully, quickly realize that you, even in the present state of the Expansion of your Light, can become a Blazing Sun of Light wherever you move!

To our Beloved Children of the Light who are soon to go to Norway, We thank you for carrying the Light there. Remember you are rendering a transcendent Service. We watch the blessed ones going here and there, and those who stand so loyally to this Instruction which Saint Germain has brought forth. Great will be that Blessing to them. See how quickly everything comes into Divine Order and is so sustained!

Watch! Be alert, O Precious Children of the Light! Silence every discord and inharmony that attempts to find expression in your world, either through yourself or outside. Then you will find great calm, peace, and serenity filling your world, filling your Heart, until when you call there will quickly come the Answer from the "Presence." The Messengers have pled with you to do this, for there is the imperative need of harmony and stillness in your feelings. Once you realize this, you will find that in the stillness there will come *always* — quickly and clearly — the Answer required. It cannot fail! Oh, Beloved Ones, do you think that your "Presence," the Governor of the Universe, could fail? Do you not see how incredible such a thing would be, and that it is only the human concept which longer prevents you from entering quickly into the Freedom which the "Presence" is?

Believe, oh, Precious Ones, the experiences of this Good Brother on Mount Shasta, where the Light descended rendering a Service so great! There is not one in this room — and this is no exaggeration — there is not one in this room, through whom that same Service might not be rendered. I tell you, Precious Ones, your "Presence" is not limited to Its Activity in and through you, except by your feeling world. If you will feel the *Full Authority* and Power of your "Presence" and then just be still, you will quickly find that this "Presence" is a never-failing Release of all that is required.

The happiness within your feeling is the great Golden Key which the Light of your being turns, and the Door opens into your Freedom. In the "Presence" is all you require — not yet, possibly, in outer manifested form! But the pattern or idea, the Intelligence for its perfect manifestation in any required form is there, within the conscious acceptance of your "Presence" into your feeling world.

We wish all might feel this so clearly, so freely. Now, during the remainder of the time that I am speaking to you, because We always endeavor to render at least one Service during a given period, will you not feel with Me *everything* within your being that has bound or limited you, *let go!* I say: *"All human creation that has limited or bound these Children of Light, LET GO! All human creation that has limited or bound these Children of Light, LET GO NOW! and be replaced by the full Power and Perfection of their 'Mighty I AM Presence'—in full Power and Action!"* We accept this in the full Power of Its Activity for every blessed one, and qualify It to be eternally sustained in this Mighty Activity. Please, in your mental and feeling world, *accept that this human creation is fully silenced.*

From each Great Focus of Light in the atmosphere of Earth there are being released Mighty Currents of Energy to help mankind set themselves free. One comes from that Mighty Ancient Focus in South America, the Great Province of Peru, which once knew such Great Light in its outward expression. The Great Light, oh, Beloved Ones, is still there and ere long will stream forth in three Great Rivers of Light. The World, in spite of its appearance, is being bathed in the Glory of God, the "Mighty I AM Presence"; and ere long, hundreds of thousands will know their "Mighty I AM Presence."

In Norway We once met many of those Great Beings of Light whose Province it is to assist the Children of Earth. We, seeing that this Knowledge of the "I AM" is reaching so near Our Great Focus once held there—I take this opportunity to thank those who will go forth and expand It to those people. In their quiet of the past months, I want them to know it has been for the building up of Energy to go forth in this service. May this blessed trinity rejoice.

I wish tonight that I might talk Heart to Heart with each one of you and cause you to feel My Heart throb in that which I know is being quickened into action for you. As Beloved Saint Germain's Joy has been so great recently, so too are We feeling and pouring out to you Our Joy, that you have the simplicity of expression which brings such majestic action. In the simple words, "the Power of your Attention," do you not see, oh, Precious Ones, that it is the *simplicity of thought and expression which brings the great release of the Powers of Freedom?* Only in the complication of expression is the Truth so often hidden. Ever shall Saint Germain be blessed for bringing this Knowledge of the "Mighty I AM Presence" forth in such simple language that all may understand and apply It. So We are blessing Him as greatly as you are, for that Great, Great Service He has rendered.

You know, sometimes you are not always obedient. Sometimes We are not — in this way: Saint Germain has asked that We refrain from commending Him. Chananda said last night to Saint Germain, "I am sorry to disappoint you, but I have got to do it." So you see, We too are sometimes disobedient; but We too call on the Law of Forgiveness and try to do better the next time! So will you not feel with Us such great Joy and Happiness? Could you conceive of anything that would give Us such Great Happiness as to see the Expansion of your Light and the Freedom that awaits you so near at hand? Oh, it is no longer a long drawn-out activity. Just forget that part of it! It is not long any more. Just rejoice — oh, with so great a rejoicing — in every day calling the Power of your "Mighty Presence" into action to cleanse, to purify your mind, body, world, and your homes!

Oh, those homes! Oh, what a feeling! — what a feeling is in the word "home"! Every home in the World in outer manifestation should be a Sacred Altar of God in Action. What a World — what a Heaven on Earth that would be! Oh, for that day! Do not feel Me critical when I say this, but, oh, for that day when once again mankind — notice this expression — is unpiled from on top of each other. Then they will not worry whether their "Mighty I AM Presence" is in someone else's apartment! However, I would advise all not to worry about that, even in the present state. Let the "Presence" take care of it. You may be sure the "Mighty I AM Presence" is quite able to take care of Itself.

We see from Our Great Field of Activity the vicinity of Lake Titicaca, from which one day shall be released again Its Great Powers. Many of you will see and know this of which I speak. Remember that not so far from this Great Focus of Light there was one of the greatest destructive activities on the Earth. There are caves in Our Beloved Andes where one day there was broken up the greatest focus of darkness on the Earth. In that age, the final battle was won between the Light and darkness. *The Light of course always wins; and so It will again in your Beloved America—in Our Beloved America.*

In your song tonight you touched deeply within My Heart. Hence, Great is My Joy to have been present with you and rendered a Service which it is My Privilege to give. May I remind you, just at this point, how great is this uplifting activity, how great is your happiness when you have rendered some service to each other out here in your world of action! Then can you just imagine for a moment Our Great Joy when We find an opportunity, sometimes even to Us wholly unexpected, to render a Service sometimes very far-reaching. *Tonight it is far-reaching, from the Andes to the Sierras!* Does that sound like a long distance! Well, it is not! That is the human concept which says so. To Us who have forgotten, so far as Our own Activity is concerned, that there is time and space, is it any wonder We feel there is no distance? It is possible for everyone to become so conscious of his "Mighty I AM Presence" that he has no cognizance of time and space. To feel it, or to be so imbued with this feeling that you go through the activities of a whole day as though it were an hour or perhaps a few minutes, is joy unspeakable.

You know how often in your contemplation of the "Presence," one, two, or three hours pass and it seems but a few minutes? That is a slight intimation to you of what it really means to transcend time and space. The Great Cosmic Law is now permitting this to be done more and more for the Children of Earth. Thus It is hastening, quickening powerfully, your own Call for the Freedom of all mankind. You who are privileged to know your "Mighty I AM Presence" in this way, will find yourselves a Thousand-Petaled Lotus, Its Thousand Rays reaching out everywhere to bless, to heal, to prosper and enlighten.

Our Precious Lotus! We thank and bless her for her ceaseless Service and her great happiness in that Service. I shall, for one, stand by and see that she never lacks for energy and strength. Your love is oh so great, pouring out to her, and I thank you with deepest Gratitude. Notice, Dear Hearts, how the great earnest Call to the "Mighty I AM Presence" dissolves and clears away all mist of human creation. A great number of the earnest "I AM" Students are fast surging forward, into a great Peace at first—then the feeling of their Mastery over their worlds, then the feeling of a great Love and Kindliness pouring out to all mankind, which opens every Door before them into whatever activity is required.

Oh, Precious Ones, do you not see that those who have felt jealous and inharmonious just fade out of the Light—blaming others, when only within themselves is the fault? Oh, Precious Ones, so many of these are precious ones whose Light is very great; but when they become caught in that snare of jealousy, criticism, or condemnation, their own blessed Door just closes temporarily and they feel alone in the world. I, with you tonight, call to the "Mighty I AM Presence" of each one of those precious ones who have for one reason or another allowed themselves to feel unkind to the Messengers, or critical: " 'Mighty I AM Presence,' dissolve once and forever every human creation about them—cause and effect—and set those blessed ones free in the Light, that they may have the Freedom which is so near them."

If only mankind and the precious Students could see that the moment a discordant feeling stirs within them, it is just the sinister, human creation which would bind them longer in their limitations and distress. Oh, that all might understand this and be so firm in their refusal to speak or accept from others any inharmonious expression! Then their worlds would quickly be at peace, filled with the Glory of the "Presence" and the abundance of every good thing they require for use in the Service of the Light.

The God Tabor, the God Himalaya, and the God from the Swiss Alps join Me in pouring forth tonight a fourfold Activity for your Blessing, for your Freedom. May I ask you to accept the fullness of It to go forth and do Its Perfect Work for you?

We love you, We thank you, We bless you.

SAINT GERMAIN'S DISCOURSE

ROGERS' GROUP — LOS ANGELES, CALIFORNIA

JANUARY 24, 1937

MY PRECIOUS Children of the Light, you are My happy Family! Justly I can claim this, for great happiness has entered into your world. It is building each day with a Glory and certainty in the Onrush of the Light in, through you, and out into your world. Oh, it is so much greater than yet you quite realize. Tonight while We have a little Heart-to-Heart talk, will you not feel entering into your being and world a Mighty Activity—first, of the Quality of Peace and Rest; then of a Mighty Activity so powerful that anything you have previously conceived would sink into insignificance in comparison with it, for such is the Truth!

You have gained a power and momentum now in calling your "Mighty I AM Presence" into action. Will you allow Us to help you in this Explanation We offer? Precious Ones, this is far more important than you realize; for when We ask you to accept a Quality, you are really accepting a Substance containing that Quality, which makes It constantly active within your being and world.

I do not feel that it is necessary to longer prompt

27

you concerning any wrong activity, but rather to encourage you in the Strength of your "Mighty I AM Presence," to flood your world with such a Glory that you wholly forget there is anything else. We never prompt beyond a certain point, but you will remember what was said to you in the Shrine Class: now, the Great Cosmic Law does permit Us to fight some of your battles for you. I do not mean by that, you are to lie down on the job. You must make your Application with firm determination—firmer than ever for the next few months; but the Great Cosmic Law does permit Us to give you Assistance—which We always stand ready to do—and that is your great privilege at this time.

Never, now notice this, *never* in My Experience have I, or any of the other Ascended Masters, known such great Assistance to be given, or such an Opportunity in the Action of the Great Cosmic Law. This means a very long time, for I have definitely consciously ministered to bless all mankind during many centuries. Let us take it from the seventy thousand period. Seventy thousand years is a long time according to the human sense, and yet you Blessed Ones get discouraged in a few weeks or a few months! Well, I will not say I was not discouraged during that time; but still I was able to surmount it, if that was the case. So are you Precious Ones being able to surmount anything that confronts you, because of your

"Presence" which gives you Life and beats your Hearts.

Think of it, Dear Hearts, any moment that your courage wavers, just stop a moment, still yourself, and think: "What nonsense! My 'Mighty I AM Presence' is giving me Life with which I think and speak and move about. Therefore, I give It the full Power to take command in my world and produce Perfection." Then, just become still and get your human self out of the way a little more. Do you not see, that is the principal thing required? If you could only make the human be still and let the "Presence" flood forth to do it, It would of Its own Volition do the things you require and ask It to do. You must accept your "Presence." Use your ability and authority to call your "Presence" into action to produce certain results. Then do you not see how very much greater are the results, than if you did not know of your "Presence"?

Do you not see how tremendous your Call to the "Presence" is and what it means in the quickness of the Freedom which you are seeking? That is the beauty of it. Oh, the wonder of it, Precious Ones! To think you have come to know an Invincible "Presence" which actually beats your Heart, whose Intelligence is limitless, whose Powers are limitless, whose Powers are Universal! It will answer your Call—every detail of it—gladly, joyously, and freely, only asking you one thing: to keep your feelings harmonized *enough* so you do not requalify the Great Stream of powerful, Perfect Energy which is flowing in at your Call. Just let It go forward into your world, to harmonize and produce Its Perfection there.

It is wonderful you are getting this more powerfully than ever in your Life tonight, and I rejoice with you exceedingly. Your "Presence" cannot fail in anything, oh, My Precious Ones. Your Call, if you were an invalid in bed—your Call is as powerful to the "Presence" as one who is a muscular giant. Will you not feel this Great Truth—this Mighty Truth? If you could only whisper to your "Presence" your need and then abide in it, It would rush Its Power forth to do that which was required.

Please, you Precious Ones here who have now gained this momentum, do not ever feel that anyone has any more power than you to call your "Mighty I AM Presence" into Action to flood your world with Perfection, to solve any problem, and release to you the supply you require. Oh, it is the Truth. It is only when you get discouraged that you momentarily seem to shut the Door, but even in that you really do not. You have only just stayed the momentum a little. Then again, as you enter into the Joy of that Great Perfection of the "Presence," again It will flood forth with Its great Joy of Achievement. It is so very beautiful.

I suppose I am going to get a little sentimental again tonight; but Dear Hearts, how We do love you Precious Ones! When I see the great earnestness, your great determination to have your Freedom, and the wonderful Application which you are making, I just long to take you in My Arms and whisper in your ear, "Go on, My Blessed One, you are gaining your complete Victory." Oh, many times, Dear Hearts, when you least expect it, I do whisper in your feelings that wonderful Courage and Strength.

There are those in this room tonight who will go forth imbued with such Power and Strength that nothing will ever stop them again or even seem to. They will go forward in the Strength of their "Mighty I AM Presence," amplified by the Great Host of Ascended Masters. They will feel forever sustained by the Mighty Glory of their "I AM Presence," as the full commanding Activity, the Light of the World and, oh, I rejoice!

There are many of you to whom I wish I might speak individually; but you must feel My Feeling in your Hearts, because you are doing so wonderfully. All of you are doing so wonderfully. When I see the great change that has taken place in New York and Philadelphia, it is wonderful. I see how the blessed Students of Cincinnati and those various places in the East where We were so recently, are standing like Generals in the Call to the "Presence" in this present need [recent flood conditions]. It is a very wonderful thing, and I rejoice tremendously with them.

There are many things which I wish I might say to you tonight; but you are not yet quite sufficiently in position, to do so. I say to you: glorious and wonderful things are before you who will stand determinedly and call your "Presence" into action firmly. To you the very Gates of Heaven, so-called, will open.

If you could see with the Inner, True All-Seeing Eye the difference in your city when the Messengers first came here, and now today—from the Inner standpoint it is perhaps one of the most amazing things anyone ever witnessed. You are transforming and changing the whole city. You will see the evidence of it in many, many ways. Go on and on and on, oh, My Precious Ones, individually and in Groups. Go on with your wondrous Mighty Work.

I am just going to reverse the Call with you tonight. You have been calling Us to come forth. I say to you tonight, you could not want Us half as much to come forth in the Tangible, Visible Form as We should love to come. That time is approaching, and remember: We dare not come forth and requalify powerfully your energy, until you have Self-control *enough* not to requalify it! This is all that stands between us. So keep on with your good work, and you will eventually find that you have complete Self-control. Then We can come forth the same as the Messenger stands before you tonight, and will he not be a happy chap then?

You know, Precious Ones, since the beginning of the Shrine Class We have drawn more closely into your physical world of activity by far than ever before. Now that means a great deal.

I want you to all feel Our Indomitable Courage within you which just sends you forward like a rocket in all achievement, even in the small details of your outer life. Oh, just feel the Glorious Joy from the "Presence" surging forth to do things—and when you get there, all is right! Just feel It in the morning when you get up. Hold your arms to the "Presence" and say: " 'Mighty I AM Presence,' I feel the Glory of Your Energy, Health, and Strength today. Charge them forth into my world; send them everywhere; harmonize and bring everything into Perfect Condition, and when I physically arrive see that all is prepared. See that there is only joy, harmony, and successful achievement when I arrive in physical form." Oh, Precious Ones, if you would only do that, there would not be a single thing touch you during the day.

It fills Me with such Joy when I think of the blessed Sindelars and their courage—how they have gone forth putting out the Magazine so beautifully and wonderfully, standing against a great avalanche. I see the blessed Rogers who have stood pouring forth so great a love that they cannot get places large enough to hold the people. I thank and bless the many Group Leaders—the blessed Ratana, Stanley, and the blessed Frank Lanning—all those blessed ones who have their Groups and are having such joy in drawing them together. Oh, it is so wonderful. We bless all the Group Leaders who are sincere everywhere. They are all doing a wonderful work and We rejoice so greatly in it.

Let Me remind you, because it is so wonderful— and you must not mind if We do remind you of this point often, because as you near it, oh, what tremendous things it means in your life—to think when you have served the Light enough, the Light turns and serves you! Is that not one of the most wonderful things in all the Universe? It has only required a short time in your conscious Call to your "Presence"; but suppose it were two years, suppose it were five, suppose it were ten that it was necessary for you to call your "Presence" into action to gain the point where, in your Service to the Light, It turns and begins to serve you! Is it not worth every effort the human being can make to reach this point? So many are nearing it!

Remember, in your earnest Call, that the Law of your being is—being the creator of the discord and limitations in the outer world, you must through self-conscious Call to the "Presence" dissolve and consume it. When you have made enough Application, you come to a certain point—now notice this point tonight—you come to the point where the Ascended Masters say: "You have fought the battle up to this time; now We shall take a hand and fight the battle for you." Think of it! Do you fully comprehend, Precious Ones, what that means? It means such Assistance as the average individual does not comprehend its importance to them as yet. Remember the power of your attention, Precious Ones!

This is one reason why I call your attention in these Heart-to-Heart talks to these certain things, because when your attention is upon a thing, then the thing can be fully accomplished; but how can you know a thing if your attention is not upon it? Do you not see? In the outer world you cannot know a thing until your attention is upon it. You cannot even become aware of it; because if your attention is not upon it, even the intellect will sidetrack the feeling, even though what you want is trying to get through your feeling. Your intellect will say, "Oh, that is something else."

It is marvelous, Precious Ones, to realize and watch your feelings to see what is accurate and what is not. Finally, you will find that you will be able to recognize the accurate promptings from the "Presence," just as definitely as you would distinguish a blue pencil from a white one. It is training, Precious Ones, that you need, and is what you are going through.

You are getting this training to make you alert to the Inner promptings of the "Presence," through your Higher Mental Body—making you quick and alert by Its Action through the Inner, Wondrous Prompting.

This Good Brother rejoices in this one thing, perhaps more than any particular thing; for there are times when some outer thing requires attention, and yet in the midst of it the great Inner Power begins to surge forth. Then he can do more in one day than he could ordinarily do in a week. It is a joyful, wonderful thing to feel the Power surge through with this speed and do everything—not a single move out of place—until many things are accomplished. Is that not wonderful? It can be just the same with all you Precious Ones. This is why We say, call your "Mighty I AM Presence" into action to make you alert to this Prompting and feel always ready and alert.

Oh, Precious Ones, do not keep your system too full of food. Beloved Ones, would you actually believe Me when I say that most of the "I AM" Students are still eating twice as much as they need? Actually it is true. You might think I have been around sometimes. I might have been, and it is not eavesdropping either; but Our Love is so great for you, Dear Hearts, that We want to give everyone all the Freedom We can, and help you in the quickest manner possible. I do not mean you should starve yourselves—that would

be a great extreme — but do not continue to eat, Dear
Hearts, until you feel uncomfortable. Just stop a little
before that. You know, I have recently been thinking
that I shall have to take this Good Brother in hand,
too.

Do you know this is a thing that does happen many
times? You go into an atmosphere where people are
very hungry, and you will take on the same feeling
if you do not watch out and guard against it. Now
believe it or not, that is true and is why many people
who are sensitive eat more than they really want!
Watch out for this feeling, when you are eating where
there are a great number of people — in cafeterias and
places of that kind. In these places, some of the
people may not have had so much to eat for a few
days. When they come in and you happen to touch
their atmosphere, you who are sensitive might easily
take on that feeling. Then when you go out, you
wonder why you ate so much. Do you see?

I tell you, Precious Ones, once you understand how
to guard yourself against all human suggestions, you
will feel a freedom indescribable; for it is one of the
most wonderful things in the world.

Do you not see, Precious Ones, you are moving in
an atmosphere charged dynamically with human
suggestions of every conceivable description? If you
do not call the "Presence" to hold Its Guard about
you, the human feeling rides in and qualifies you and

your world with its activity. I am only mentioning this one thing tonight; but there are dozens of things—feelings of mankind—which you will register if you do not stand guard and refuse acceptance to all human feelings. Unless you call your "Presence" to stand guard, you will, at least temporarily, be inclined to carry them out. It is the same thing, Dear Hearts, with anger, with irritation, with sex conditions or whatever it is.

For instance, you go into the streetcar and sit down by one whose idea is charged with one of those things. If you do not refuse acceptance and call your "Presence" to protect you, you will take on that feeling and think it is your own. This is why many people find such difficulty in correcting and dissolving the sex desire—because they come into the atmosphere of people in which that feeling is so heavily charged, and they begin to accept it into their feelings unknowingly. Outwardly, there may be nothing in the individual that would indicate it; but the feeling is acting just the same.

Oh, Dear Hearts, I tell you, "I AM" Students, watch your feelings! I tell you, Beloved "I AM" Students, do not go to any other "I AM" Student with the feeling of sex desire in your being, as you value your progress. That thing has gone on among some of the Students. Watch out, Dear Hearts, that those do not come into your midst who are not especially interested in the "I AM," but think they see an opportunity to get their claws upon the Students. I warn you!

A Student that will go into the home of another and offer sex suggestions to anyone there is not fit to be called an "I AM" Student — and We know all that is going on! I tell you, Precious Ones, your day is short! Do not allow those things to govern you longer. If you are determined to gratify your sex in your own home, that is your own business; but do not go to any other "I AM" Student with an atmosphere charged with that desire and, either through feeling or otherwise, offer that suggestion.

I am prompting you because of so great a Love. You cannot yet possibly understand how We know all that is going on in your feeling world. We have to, Dear Hearts! How could We help you if We did not? Do you think you can be drawn into Our Radiation and We not know what is going on in your mental and feeling world? It is impossible, Dear Hearts! We do not seek it; but when you are seeking the Light, Our Radiation and Assistance, We are compelled to know what is in your feeling — not with the slightest sense of criticism or condemnation, only in loving Kindness to offer Our Assistance that We may help you to be free.

Oh, Beloved Ones, I have seen some of our blessed Students — a few only — who have been so earnest, have expressed and claimed the Great Blessing that they have received from this "I AM" Work, and then have receded into the extreme sex gratification again. I want to awaken them to what they are doing, for it just deprives them and shuts the Door of Light before them. God, the "Mighty I AM Presence," help them and set them free!

Tonight, oh, My Loved Ones, it is just like We were sitting in My Home with all you Precious Ones around Me, and We were just talking in this Heart-to-Heart manner—just as though I were answering the many questions besetting you. I feel just like that tonight in the great Love which goes out, enfolding you; for it enables Me to prompt you in these things. Know it is all in such great loving Kindness.

My Precious Ones, you are all very dear, so dear to Our Hearts. The Blessed Nada, the Beloved Master Jesus, the Great Divine Director, Chananda, Leto, and Lanto all wish to convey Their Love and Blessings to you tonight. It is just as though you were together in Their midst listening to Them. Will you not accept this—Their Blessing and Radiation in your feeling world, in your mental world, in your outer world of activity—and let Its Great Radiation go forth to give you whatever Assistance is required?

In the great stillness of this wondrously charged atmosphere is that of which you have often heard, and yet mankind has so little comprehended: "In the

Great Silence or Stillness is God's Greatest Activity."
As you have been so sweet and kind to give Me your
attention tonight, during this stillness of the outer
there has flowed into your beings Our Wondrous Substance, which will become an eternally active Presence within and for you. When you would lack in
courage, It will assert Itself and take you forward;
when you feel a little lack of energy, then It will come
into action and stimulate you to make your Call and
have Its Mighty Energy flow through.

Precious Ones, believe Me tonight when I say there
is not one of you in this room but who can raise his
hands to the "Presence" every morning when you get
up—not later than eight o'clock—and through your
Call to the "Presence" charge your mind and body
with Its Mighty Strength, Courage, Health, and Energy. Dear Hearts, if there has been the slightest intimation of any disturbance, say: " 'Mighty I AM
Presence,' pass your Violet Consuming Flame through
my mental and feeling body; sweep out and dissolve
all imperfection. Then pour Your Mighty Currents
through, filling my mind and body with Your Mighty
Health, Strength, and Buoyancy." Oh, My Precious
Ones, you can have perfect health and happiness, joyous strength and energy filling your body every day,
if you will. If the first time you do not feel the full
result, go right on and on and on; and suddenly you
will find when you make the Call, the Energy will flow

in and fill your body tremendously. You will not have to make the Call a second time that day.

Notice, you might easily and justly ask Me, "Why do I have to make the Call each day?" Because, Precious Ones, you are moving in a seething vortex of discordant feeling and suggestion from mankind, and you must keep calling to the "Presence" until you have gained the momentum to be your sustained protection. Therefore, you must keep on calling until your momentum becomes so great it acts involuntarily. Even then, until you have made the Ascension, it would be far better to continue to make your Call every day than to rest on the "Presence" and not make it. Can you not make that effort at least? You see, the inclination of all human beings, Dear Hearts, is to "let George do it." I am sure you all agree with Me that all have been inclined to let someone else do it, because "I don't feel quite like it today." That is just the time, Dear Hearts, you want to rise up and say, "Here, you cannot do this thing."

Now I tell you frankly, when you feel the slightest touch of cold, rise up and say in the full consciousness of your "Presence": "I will not have that! 'Mighty I AM Presence,' take it out of me—cause and effect! Fill me with Your Health, Strength, and Energy, and stop this nonsense." Dear Hearts, you can dismiss it in just a few minutes. If you do this a few times, you would stop that habit from acting in you, and you would feel your ability to control such conditions completely. You will dismiss it at once and not have to go through several days of such experience.

Oh, I tell you, Dear Hearts, My rejoicing is tremendous because I know you are gaining the full consciousness of this. I know your feeling, and you must understand you can do these things. You are shutting out these things with tremendously greater firmness, and preventing them from acting in your world. It was the sinister thing that started this suggestion of flu among mankind. It was nothing else in the world. It is nonsense, Dear Hearts; do not accept it into your world just because that silly suggestion starts and people succumb to it. Do you not see, it is the power of suggestion that gets them down and then treads upon them? Do not do it.

In this Good Brother's practice, I have seen him, during those years of healing, go to patients who thought they were so ill they could not raise their heads. In a half an hour they would be up and dressed. Nothing in the world was the matter with those people but the suggestion which had been driven into their consciousness. As soon as he removed that, they were all right. This is exactly what takes place with more than seventy-five percent of the conditions mankind meets. It is but suggestion. If mankind understood how to be quickly alert and on the defense, it could not register in the feeling.

This is why tonight I want to prompt you dear
"I AM" Students. I see there are several places where
some of the Groups have accepted the idea that they
have the flu. Well they have not! Just as though an
"I AM" Student could have flu! If they accept it, I
do not! And I know I am stronger than they are. I
tell you and those blessed ones everywhere in your
Groups or among your friends whom you meet, kindly
try to prompt them to stand on guard against these
things.

Now tonight, Precious Ones, until We have the opportunity to speak to you again, know that Our Love,
Blessing, and Light enfold you always. When there
is an earnest need, send forth your Call, and Help will
come at once. You see when you call to your "Mighty
I AM Presence," if outer assistance is required, it
always goes forth. Call to your "Mighty I AM Presence" first, then the Great Host of Ascended Masters
if you feel it is necessary, and Help will come. Do not
accept anything else. But best of all, stand guard every
morning; draw those Mighty Currents of Health in
to fill your body. Call the "Presence" to draw around
you the Mighty Tube of Light as an Invincible Protection, to repel everything unlike the Perfection which
It is. Then go forth in your activity of the day, a wholly
free, happy, blessed, joyous being, filled with the Glory
of the "Mighty I AM Presence" and Ascended Masters—and just know We are holding your hands all

the time; for in Our Love with which We enfold you, We are holding your hands all the time until you are free.

The Love, Blessing, and Light of the Great Host of Ascended Ones, the Legion of Light, and the Great Cosmic Beings enfold you always unto your Ascension. I thank you.

SAINT GERMAIN'S DISCOURSE

SAN FRANCISCO, CALIFORNIA

FEBRUARY 13, 1937

AFTER Our experience of more than two years, in the earnest endeavor to convey to you the Understanding of the "Mighty I AM Presence" which is your Freedom, it is most gratifying indeed, oh, Beloved Ones, to see the Expansion of the Light within your Hearts and of all the Students throughout America and the World. Again, I say, it is most gratifying to find those Books have found their way into all parts of the World, carrying their Light and their Freedom to all points of the globe.

We have been with you during the past ten days, and have with the greatest of Joy felt the loving response within your Hearts. We too rejoice exceedingly. I say this that you may know it is only the beginning of the great Joy, the great Light, the great Freedom which is yours. So many have entered into It sufficiently to know there is really no limit to that which they may attain. I say to you tonight—and I try to put into it all the Love of My Being—I congratulate you Blessed Ones in San Francisco on the Expansion of your Light, in spite of the seeming chaos which at times seemed to be in your midst. Yet, steadily and surely

46

have you gone forward, in the greater and greater Expansion and Perfection of your Presence of Life, which is your "Mighty I AM."

In your future work here, Precious Ones, remember that We are always pouring forth Our Radiance to you, where there is Harmony; but We cannot do it where there is not. To those who refuse to give obedience to the simple things We ask, We cannot give Our Radiance; for without obedience nothing can be accomplished. Furthermore, We will not release great volumes of energy into the use of anyone unless We are sure they will not requalify it with anger, criticism, hatred, or any of those qualities which are destructive.

One day you shall know how great Our Love is for you, and how earnestly We watch to guard everywhere. When the Beloved Messengers are prompted to warn and guard you, please do not feel that they are interfering with your Free Will at any time. Such is not the case, but as Messengers they must convey the Truth. Always just remember, their Love is very, very great for you, and they will stand by always to give assistance. Oh, Beloved Ones of the Light, your very Heartbeat is a throb of Delight from your "Mighty I AM Presence," giving you Life! Life! Life! more, and more, and more Life! As you gain in your understanding and feel your authority to call forth this Great Intelligent Energy from your "Mighty

I AM Presence," watch! stand guard! that you do not requalify It.

I am sure in this Class, as never before, you feel the greater and greater Reality of this Privilege which is yours in receiving from your "Mighty I AM Presence" Its limitless Intelligence, limitless Energy, and greater and greater Strength, more and more perfect Health. I say to you with full assurance that no one can fail if he has understood refusing acceptance of discordant appearances and conditions, and will earnestly call the "Presence" into Action. All must have Perfect Health. It is the Law of your being, Precious Ones, no matter what the conditions are, what the X ray shows in anyone's body. The "Presence" releases those Mighty Currents of Energy in and through the body and sweeps out every imperfection that is there. Will you accept it? Will you believe it? Let the Power flow through to bring you Perfect Health—it is essential. If you are constantly harassed by the feeling of pain and distress in the body, you cannot give your fullest attention to the "Presence," so that It releases the greatest volume. Therefore, sometimes one needs encouragement or strength; and I trust there is no "I AM" Student who comes under this Radiation that will not willingly, joyously give that.

I say to all of you, Beloved Students, never allow yourselves to be impatient with those who come to you for advice or help. Do not ever answer them impatiently, and do not ever refuse help. Do not ever say to one who comes to you: "You have an 'I AM Presence.' Why do you not stand by It?" That would be unkind. You do not know the forces playing upon that one which might have discouraged him. Instead, place your hand about that one's shoulder and say: "My brother—or my sister—my hand is in yours in the Strength of my 'Mighty I AM Presence,' until you have won your Victory. Go forth, call your 'Mighty I AM Presence' into action and I will help you." Send them forth feeling that you are interested in their Victory.

We must know all that is going on, Precious Hearts, in your lives. Do you know that? Having entered into the Radiance of your "Mighty I AM Presence" in this Knowledge which I have brought forth, you invite Us to observe your world; otherwise We cannot help. Therefore, if We see you are impatient, We try to pour forth the Radiation of Kindliness which will give you patience and strength to assist. Do not ever say anything or allow a feeling to go forth that would be discouraging.

Remember! Allow no one to come into your midst, individually or collectively, who breathes a word of discord or condemnation of this Work. If you do, you will close the Door. We do not wish you to do that, but We cannot prevent you; for everyone under this Radiation is wholly given his Free Will to choose, and always shall. We, with all the Love and Joy of Our Hearts, want to give you Freedom; but you must make your Call to your "Mighty I AM Presence" and stand by it.

Then you give Us the opportunity to—through your "Mighty I AM Presence"—intensify all activities, until you have the courage, strength, and power to resist all outer suggestions which would deprive you or detain you from your full Victory. Will you not stand so firm by your "Mighty I AM Presence" and in It, that We can always give the Assistance required, whether it is Health, Strength, Courage, or Directing Intelligence?

I say to you, all of you Precious Ones here: *Please do not accept that you cannot receive clear Directing Intelligence from your "Presence."* I have a great reason for saying this to you. There have been quite a number of Students who yet do not feel that they can call their "Presence" into action and receive the Direction clear enough to be sure. Now, Precious Ones, that is only because knowingly or unknowingly there has been some anxiety within you which has been disturbing you—disturbing the vibratory action of your being, or your nervous system.

Therefore, if you will be still and say to your "Presence": " 'Mighty I AM Presence!' You help me to be still, so that Your Directing, Intelligent Energy can get through; make me understand — through my feeling or in some manner — make me feel clearly what I should do." As you do this, you will find in some manner *directly* what is the thing to do; but watch out! Be sure you do not, in the feeling, first begin to doubt that you are going to have the Directing Intelligence from your "I AM Presence." If you do, you start that vibratory action which is discouraging, through your feelings, before you actually know it in the intellect. That feeling of yours is rather an unruly fellow, but you can govern it — *the "Presence" will!*

This time in the Class, oh, Precious Ones, so much has been accomplished. I rejoice with all My Heart and I congratulate you. You will find that you will all go forth in such a great calm Confidence and Victory from tonight, as you have not thought possible to be attained in your outer activity. We have offered to hold your hands until the Victory. May We not do it? May We not hold your hands until you are free, *wholly free from all limitations,* feeling clearly, powerfully, definitely your Victory? We shall be so happy to do it — always through the Radiation of your Wondrous "Presence." Do you not understand that We, as Ascended Beings, are One with the "Mighty I AM Presence" of you who are not yet Ascended, and that is how We must know all about you in order to give you the Assistance which is necessary.

It is so very wonderful; you must get My Feeling! With such Rejoicing, I see how you have become able to still yourselves. In this Class such a Radiance has poured forth, although you are not yet aware of it but in a small way. Do you think, Precious Ones, that the Divine Director would have come here in your midst, pouring forth these Great Currents of Energy into your minds and bodies, if He had not seen that you were able to still yourselves enough to have the full Benefit of it? His Great Wisdom would not do that unless it was time, was right, was permanent. So I congratulate you of San Francisco and those visiting here, that you called your "Mighty I AM Presence" into action which made the way open and clear for you to be here. That in itself is a great Victory. I wish you might see in the atmosphere of mankind how many blessed ones have momentarily had good intent, but been sidetracked from the Radiation by some vicious suggestion. If you saw the number who had been turned aside from this Class by the vicious suggestion from others, in which there was no Truth, you would be surprised. If that had not been the case, this lovely, blessed place could not nearly have held them. The tragedy is theirs. You who have had the strength to come in spite of all opposition, have the Victory.

Oh, that all mankind might understand how all progress is due to their own initiative. You must

choose, Precious Ones. I speak to all mankind—into
their mental and feeling world—you not only must,
but you are compelled to choose, before the greater
Energy and Power will be released to come into your
world and produce the Perfection which you wish. If
you are sitting on the fence, you will not get much
Help; but when you straighten up your spine and say:
" 'Mighty I AM Presence!' I am one hundred percent
—or one thousand percent—with *You!* Release Your
Mighty Powers into action to free me and my
world!"—do you think for one moment that Its Energy
will not come forth? Let Me tell you *It will,* and with
no uncertainty. But if there is wavering in your consciousness and doubt, do you not see that is requalifying the Energy, and It cannot do for you what It
should and what you would like to have It do? Now
many times those things are acting in the feeling of
mankind, mostly unconsciously. The individual is not
outwardly aware of it; but if you will call your
"Presence" into action, It will correct the condition.

I say to those who have been here for the first time:
It does not matter what your doubts might be; if you
would call your "Presence" into action three times
daily, earnestly, for five minutes, inside of ten days
you would have the evidence in your own experience
so strong that nothing could turn you aside. The condition is, owing to the mass creation about mankind,
that those who are not anchored, unknowingly listen

to the falsehood about them, which even turns them temporarily aside. Will you not explain this, oh, Precious Students, to those you contact who are partially interested? Because mankind does not understand the laws and forces acting upon them, they are often deprived of the great Freedom, Joy, and Blessing which is waiting for them.

The Radiance in the Class has surpassed anything so far, and I want you Precious Ones to know that. In the fullness of My Love I say to you, if you wish Us to come twice a year—this year and next—We will come to you. I say for your Blessing and Freedom, do not be worried about anything injuring this Work. All the vicious gossip there is, does not amount to anything. Those unfortunate individuals are but destroying themselves! They are not injuring you or this Work; *they cannot do it.* But the pitiful thing is that they still think they can.

I want to say to our blessed friends, the Christian Scientists: In their churches, I am amazed that people who pretend to pour forth Love, would turn in viciousness against this Love, this Radiation of the Light and the Understanding of the "Mighty I AM Presence," which is the Source of all Life. This is the first time I have spoken My Opinion; but I say today, and you may carry My Word to them, "It is pitiful!"

I tell you frankly—and you may carry this to all Christian Science churches throughout America and the World: Unless they stop that, they will destroy every church and its attendance which they now have. I say this in all Love and Kindness. I wish to stop such a thing coming on, for great good has been accomplished through Christian Science; but I tell you frankly, *every source*—whether it is Unity, Christian Science, or whatever it is—that attempts to bring disgrace upon this Work or condemns or criticizes It, will fail utterly and their churches will be empty!

This Work opposes nothing in the World. It goes on presenting this Wondrous "Presence"—the "Mighty I AM"—which every human being on Earth should be delighted to know about and understand; and because they have allowed suggestions to enter their ranks and fear that this would empty their churches, they have turned in many instances in vicious hatred to the Messengers and this Work. God alone pity them!

Unity has done the same thing, through the claw of the sinister force which has entered into their Heart center. I say this to you in all Kindness, Dear Hearts. Watch! Every source that has presented some part of the Truth which condemns this Work, will fail utterly, because the Messengers have never condemned any activity and never shall! They have presented this Mighty Law of the "I AM Presence" in their humble kindness, and if people do not wish to come into this Mighty Truth of the "I AM," they should not condemn It. I stated in the Shrine Class that the Messengers have carried forth bravely thus far and, by their powerful, dynamic Application, have held their own protection and carried the Work forth. Now then, We shall fight their battles and they shall hold their peace.

I marvel at the individuals among mankind who are too stubborn to believe the Mighty Truths recorded in *Unveiled Mysteries* and *The Magic Presence.* We never — an Ascended Being will never — use a destructive force; but mark what I tell you, as described in *Unveiled Mysteries:* the Mighty Host of Ascended Masters draw the Wall of Light, and when the viciousness of the individual strikes It, their own viciousness rebounds upon them and they must handle it — if they can.

That is the Law of everyone's being. We do not wish to harm anyone; but We shall not allow the Messengers to be harmed — nor this Work! When those within humanity have been willingly strong enough to carry forth to a certain point, then the Great Law sweeps in and takes a hand. So I say to you, Precious Ones, We love the Christian Scientists, We love all Unity, We love all mankind; but the viciousness that comes in their ranks *shall not harm these Loved Ones. Neither shall it harm the Students of the Light!* I say to you, Beloved Cora Wickham, here in San Francisco: "My Hand is in yours for your firm, unyielding stand in bringing the Light of the 'Mighty I AM Presence' to your friends, the Christian Scientists. One day you will not be able to care for them all, so many will come. Your loving Heart and kindness will render a transcendent Service and are rendering it."

Every Blessed One of the Students here and Group Leaders, I enfold you in My Love; but do not feel inharmonious to each other. Whenever a feeling of discord or inharmony comes from one Student to another or from one Group to the other, remember, you can always know instantly it is but a claw of the sinister force driving in, trying to destroy the great good you are doing.

Now you will notice, Precious Ones, the Messengers fear nothing. They are wholly unconcerned about all this silly criticism and falsehood, which is spread by individuals because they are not permitted to drive into this Heart Center of Light. I want you to understand here in San Francisco, you Blessed Ones, that We are back of you—the Great Host of Ascended Masters—and one day, you will know that *We are even more Real than you are.* One day you will know that We are not an imagination of this Good Brother. You will find that We are *very Real,* and We can be *very Tangible,* but yet still Invisible. Do not forget that!

Some of these people who have tried to claim and prove discrepancies in those marvelous Books will one day cry out for Mercy. Mark what I tell you! We bide

Our time, but mark what I tell you! We spread it to the World: *No person, place, or thing shall ever harm or destroy this Work.* It shall go on, until every one of mankind knows this "Mighty I AM Presence," and through It, all have their freedom. I say this to you tonight for your strength, courage, power, and freedom. To Us, the silly falsehood, condemnation, and criticism is silly nonsense and has no power.

Remember, Precious Ones! To every appearance that is less than the Perfection of the "Presence," say, "You have no power!" Mean it in your feelings, and you will have no trouble entering your world or disturbing you. It is true, absolutely true, the appearances or discordant forces in mankind have no power, except the thought and feeling which goes into them and feeds them with the Life of the individual.

Look, Precious Ones, in your recent airplane accidents. Do you not see that from everything which has such an appearance, a momentum goes forth? If it had not been for the Decrees which the blessed Students of America have given, that thing would have gained a momentum, until a dozen or more planes would have been destroyed. The sinister force wants just such a thing to start so mankind may not be in close contact. I thank the Messengers and the Students for issuing the Decrees to protect the Radio, because there has been a deliberate attempt which would try to interfere with the Radio in America and the World;

but it shall not do it! I tell you, My Precious Ones, in your Mighty Decrees giving this Protection for various activities, you are rendering a Service that will go down through Eternity. Then one day, when you are farther progressed in your Life, you will see the Service rendered and the great intense Protection which has been given America and the great industries. Precious Ones, you have no idea how those marvelous Decrees have gone forth to solve these conditions of strikes throughout America. *Go on with your Decrees. Call the Mighty "Presence" into Action, that they may never have another strike.* Call Divine Justice to take place between the men and capital — between so-called labor and capital. There is no labor! There is only one thing — a Divine Service. Beloved Ones, please feel this in your outer activity of the world, and you will release yourselves from the feeling of labor or bondage. Wherever you are, whatever you are doing, you are serving this Great "I AM Presence" to your Freedom. Try to feel this, and let it take from you all feeling of being in the bondage of labor.

You heard what Mrs. Ballard, our Beloved Messenger, read you tonight of My Activities, which are rather the directing of Great Currents of Great Forces and Energy than taking any part in the political activity. So it is. But *America shall go forward! All official places shall be filled with the Power of Divine Justice, and great harmonious Activity shall enter into*

America and hold Its Dominion here. Mark what I tell you!

Do not, I plead with you, longer give power to appearances of anything—whether it is in the government or your individual lives. Say to every appearance: "You have no power! 'Mighty I AM Presence,' sweep into it! Produce Your Perfection and hold Your Dominion there—Your Mighty Directing Intelligence!" My Precious Ones, *you can render a Service unparalleled in the history of the World!* Will you not do it for your freedom and the freedom of mankind?

I rejoice in the strength and power which is coming within many of the Students—that strength drawn of the acceptance of the "Mighty I AM Presence," which makes them a Mighty Pillar of Light, moving through the world and spreading Its Radiance everywhere. So I congratulate every earnest Student throughout America and the World. I pour forth a Mighty Radiance to them for strength, courage, and power to go forward victorious in whatever their choice of activity is, that they may fill the World with the Beauty, Harmony, and the Glory of the "Mighty I AM Presence" in action.

In the fullness of My Love I enfold you, oh, Beloved Students, with My Courage, with My Strength, with My Perfect Health, filling your minds and bodies until there is not a vestige of anything but Love and Harmony there—if you will allow Me. We have now gone into the Heart of the "Mighty I AM Presence," the Ruler of the Universe! Let us abide there and let Its Heart act through these humble forms, that they may become electrified into the fullness of the Conquering Presence of the "Mighty I AM"! Stand forth in Its great calm serenity, realizing, feeling that God, the "Mighty I AM Presence," is henceforth their Director, their Victory in whatever choice their service might be.

GREAT DIVINE DIRECTOR'S DISCOURSE

ROGERS' 100% GROUP — LOS ANGELES, CALIFORNIA

MARCH 18, 1937

BELOVED Students of My Heart, how I rejoice that I may be instrumental in expanding, or assisting to expand, the Light within your Heart which is increasing so beautifully. Since you took part in this closed Group, the rapidity of the Expansion of your Light has been so marked that I hold My Hand up to you in gratefulness for the service rendered. You will all know it is a rare privilege when you understand what this has meant, in the willingness with which you have joyously entered into this Service. It is the greatest accomplishment so far. Many of you feel and know it in your feeling world and rejoice.

Notice this, Dear Ones, all of you who have entered into this Great Special Stream of Life and Energy — I shall tell you what your willingness has done. In entering into this Special Service, the Great Ones from Venus, who have been the Vanguard of the humanity of Earth so many hundreds of thousands of years, have accepted your Service. Do you realize, oh, Beloved Ones, what that means to Our Beloved Saint Germain? He saw and had the Courage to step forth, assuring all of Us that there were those who could carry this Message successfully—that it must be done now or never if the Earth and its humanity were to survive. Then there had to be someone found who could carry this Message, and it was achieved. Now the Great Work has gone forth; and as this Good Brother has said to you so many times, he found that in your midst today there is an opportunity to render a Service which only the Ascended Masters yet fully understand. Your being willing to serve joyously has made you a part of that Great, Great Light. Will you not feel tonight, while I speak to you, this Great Reality? You made yourselves Ambassadors of that Light, and in It you have the privilege of not only allowing, but calling forth the Light of your "Mighty I AM Presence" to spread Its Radiance everywhere you move. Think what it means as you move about among mankind!

Oh, often you move among conditions which are so discordant, and yet that Radiance, even without a spoken word, is going forth. Oh, Precious Ones, you cannot imagine how great It is. That Radiance is going forth at your charged Call—notice! *your charged Call*—because the momentum you gain from your constant Call to your "Mighty I AM Presence" becomes a *charged Call,* a charged activity, going forth everywhere, spreading Its Radiance.

I know you do not yet see this in its fullness,

physically speaking, but I see that Radiance going forth vividly, powerfully, clearly. Some of you would be gratefully surprised and even astonished to know how clearly and powerfully your Radiance is going forth from your human forms. Tonight I want to give you My Encouragement, My Strength and Energy to electrify you into the *full feeling* of the immensity of the work which you are doing.

Oh, Beloved Ones of the Light, you have heard so often why there is the need of your Call to the "Mighty I AM Presence," in order to give Us the privilege of releasing the Power and amplifying your earnest, sincere efforts to go forth and do the work required in the world—the outer as well as the mental and feeling world of mankind. Your Call *is* showing its activity throughout the Earth.

We hope ere long—if not before, by the time the Messengers return from the East—We shall have something very wonderful to convey to you. It looks today as if We would. I hope with all My Heart that We may be able to convey that to you which We wish. Then your Hearts will leap with joy unspeakable for having been a part of this Service.

The human creation of mankind has so bound blessed humanity that only now are they bursting those binding chains of their own creation. They are beginning to stand forth within the Great Light. Today, among your wondrous businessmen of the outer world, there is coming a great desire to stand in and for the Light. As these Blessed Books have gone forth spreading their Radiance and Truth, oh, how many feel the Great Truth and Wonderful Reality which they convey! This last issue of the Magazine which has the Chart will spread over the entire Earth.

Blessed Ones, great, great is your privilege in being in the vanguard of this Service which will one day set America and the World free. It will one day bring the longed-for condition upon Earth when all mankind shall be at peace and all struggle ceases. Oh, can you not feel, even as I speak the Words, the Joy, the Reality of living in such a World? It has existed many times before and will exist again—this time permanently—for the Earth. Is it not well worth every effort which mankind can make, to once again find that established on Earth?

I want you to feel tonight My Great Love and Gratitude to this Group who have rendered such great Service. I speak to you individually for a moment. Do you realize what your being willing to serve really means? Individually, it is setting you free with great speed. I plead with you Dear Hearts who have not or do not quite feel your financial freedom yet—oh, please, do not be discouraged. You cannot fail to have your supply! Please believe Me when I say this to you, for you are so near your freedom. Go on and on and on calling your "Mighty I AM Presence" into action, realizing that your Mighty "Presence" which gives you Life is the Treasure House of the Universe—your Treasure House—to whom you can call and have what you require released tonight. Everyone in this room who has not yet been able to feel this full Reality of your financial freedom, please take advantage of this opportunity and allow Me to assist you to have that full Feeling right now!

I call the "Mighty I AM Presence" forth to dissolve every doubt and question in your feeling of your ability to call the "Presence" into action to have this released right now. Please feel, as I speak to you, the Power of My own Accomplishment, to enter into your consciousness and world and give you My Feeling, the True Feeling of your financial release now—*at once*—and forever; that you may go forth from this room tonight, Master of your financial world, whether you have a cent in your pocket or not. Your "Mighty I AM Presence" holds the wealth of the Universe ready to release into your hands, when once you can remove the doubts, fears, and unbeliefs in your feeling, of the Power of your "Presence" to release it into your hands and use. Your "Presence" governs all channels in the World. Oh, please do not doubt and let your human intellect cause you to feel the unreality of your "Presence."

Your Higher Mental Body, Precious Ones, which knows the Perfection of the "Presence" and knows your needs, *will* answer your every Call, and does answer it. But watch out that in your feeling world there is not a lurking doubt which is obstructing the way—or the feeling of your inability to call your "Presence" into Action! It only requires your earnest, sincere Call! Keep it up, until you have the Power of your "Presence" acting everywhere. There is nothing in the world to stop It! It knows no resistance or in- terference, and you shall have the Power and the Freedom which It holds for you.

Please accept this tonight, and let every one of you go forth from this room filled with the Electri- fying Consciousness and Acceptance of your "Mighty I AM Presence"—your Treasure House—releasing from this moment all the money you require through the Power of Divine Love, whether it be direct or through channels, to supply you and give you the happiness and comfort which you require to render the service which your Heart desires.

There is only one obstruction to the Perfection which the "Presence" holds and that is in your *feel- ing world*. Remember what the Messenger has said to you so many times. If your Application is not pro- ducing the results you require, then say: " 'Mighty I AM Presence,' take out of my feeling world every single thing that seems to obstruct the way, and release Your Mighty Intelligent Energy to go forth and produce these Results. 'Mighty I AM Presence,' see that this is done now!" What could stand before that Great and Mighty "Presence," the Governor of the Universe? *Feel it deeply* tonight, while this opportunity is here! Oh, Blessed Ones, *feel it! feel it! feel it!*

Beloved Ones, it will be My Privilege to either be present each night when this Group meets, or send My Direct Radiance into the room for this Special Work which is being done—and for that Special Work which I wish to do, with your permission, for each one of you who has had the courage to step forth and join this 100% Group. It is not that We love others less—oh, not at all. We love all so greatly; but you who are willing to do this, are you not entitled to a Special Service? Would you not give a Special Service to one serving you who was willing to comply with the requirements? Do you not often give a bonus to those who have served well and unusually? Then why should We not offer an added Service to those who are willing to comply with that which We know blesses them beyond words to express? Therefore, it is My Privilege, and I offer to give you a Special Service and Assistance in this Group because you have been willing to do as We have requested.

We pour forth Our Radiance to all Groups who are sincere; but in this it is Our Privilege to give a

Special Service. If I wanted to give you a white silk handkerchief and someone else wanted to give you a blue one, is it not My Privilege? So I want you to feel how really close We have become. Oh no, no! We are not a way off somewhere anymore. Oh no! We are right here with you, holding your hands to your Victory. Will you not let Us? You know, We cannot go chasing you around to hold your hands; but We are willing to hold them to your Victory.

Oh, Beloved Ones, tonight your Hearts are beating with Mine. Do you realize that? I am sure you do; but just the same your Hearts are beating with Mine tonight. Will you feel it and ask your "Mighty I AM Presence" to qualify it eternally sustained for you? *(silence)* Have you thought, Precious Ones, how very wonderful and marvelous has been this experience tonight? Those two Precious Ones are voicing the Great Truth over the radio and in the song which is going forth; and these two blessed brothers here rendering this service—had you thought how very wonderful that is?

Oh, how very wonderful it is, Precious Ones, when personalities and personal desires can be set aside for the Great Service of the Light. One day, you shall all know what those Words mean. As the blessed ones in the Staff have been willing to serve, and their families have been willing to let them serve in so happy and joyous a manner, is it not an unheard of thing in the history of the World? Our blessed Mr. Crouse is serving all joyously and wonderfully while his family is here; our blessed Mary Ketcham from West Palm Beach serving with such devotion and power. Dear Ones, do you not see? I but mention these things to show you how wonderful it is when we can set aside personal desires for the Great Light. When we do that, shortly we find things opening before us, wherein a Great Service can be rendered.

Today, you Blessed Ones who have outer work to attend to, also have this privilege in the great unparalleled Service which you have in issuing these Decrees, which have been going forth for mankind. Do you see how no one is deprived of any good thing when rendering a transcendent, marvelous Service which is, from the human standpoint, indescribable? It is possible for the human of every one of you to be sufficiently dissolved, so you will feel the flood of your "Mighty I AM Presence" filling yourself and your world. Oh, the joy!—for it is so like the experience of this Good Brother, whose anxiety and fear was so great in those earlier years. Today, it does not exist—and so it is with you.

Ere long you will find that no appearance of limitation or discord will have any effect whatever upon you. You will just say to it: "Oh, run along, you have had your day! Do not bother me." Precious Ones, it is with a joyous dismissal of the human appearances that you find your Mastery. It is not in resistance, but with just that sort of indifference, say: "Oh, you human appearance, you have no power! Run along now! Do not try to bother me any more. You are just wasting your time." As you take that marvelous attitude to those appearances which not very long ago were so terrifying, it becomes, oh, so wonderful.

This Beloved Brother wants you to feel his Freedom—oh, so much. See how in such a short time a great transformation can take place. So it is within each one of you. I say, *"each one of you,"* Dear Hearts—everyone who is here! The rapid change is taking place! The human is dissolving—it has to! I command it to do so and set you free forever!

Will you believe Me when I say I shall long remember this evening? Surely, you too will always remember it, when once you come to understand how all takes place from within out, in this Great Activity and Acknowledgment of the "Mighty I AM Presence"—not from without in. Therefore, it is always amusing to Me when I touch upon this point with Students, because sometimes they think they are still having a struggle—while to Me, that is all past. Do you just get My Meaning? To Me your struggles are all past! I am not speaking in riddles. Remember, to Me your struggles are all past! Accept it, will you not?

Would you believe that sometimes We are

tempted? Shall I tell you how? The temptation is so great to extend My Hand and just lift you up. It could be done! I say that because it is true, so I may try to convey to you the Accomplishment.

The Radiance released in this room tonight from yourselves is the most astonishing thing you ever witnessed, if you were to suddenly see It. That is what it means, oh, Beloved Ones, to be obedient. Do you think there is anyone in the world who could possibly think that obedience to the Great Divine Law meant privation of any kind? Oh, how could anybody in the world think such a thing? Yet some of humanity do. They think that being obedient means they are going to be deprived of some of their sense desires. It will be well indeed when all these sense desires, all limitations, are bound forever. Does anyone want to hang on to them? I think not! This is why I say to you, Beloved Ones who have taken this step, keep on, go on, to your Glorious, Wondrous Freedom.

Saint Germain insisted that I speak to you tonight. I convey His Love and that from the Blessed Nada, the Blessed Master Jesus, the Beloved Lanto from the Royal Teton, and that Group of Ascended Masters in Arabia. They see among you those to whom they can give Great Assistance, and I convey Their Love and Blessing to you.

Dear Hearts, you who have entered into this 100%

Group, please do not ever accept one word, one thought, that We are not Real—that the Ascended Masters are not Real. We are far more Real than you are yet; for in that feeling of Our Reality, of Our Closeness, it enables you to become like Us. Do you know I just love to feel your Heart beat. When My Rays of Light go from My Heart to yours, then you become a part of Me—not the Messenger you see before you—but of MYSELF; and do you know that for some time this has been going on?

Oh, I want you to feel, Beloved Ones, We are no long-faced individuals; We are filled with Joy and Happiness—that serene, clean, pure Joy and Happiness which is always bubbling over. Our Gratitude is so great, even in Our Attainment—a Gratitude so great to the Principle of Life which We enjoy, of which We are a part, in which today We have become a Perfected Part. This is what We want to do—to help to assist you to become that which WE ARE.

I suppose We must consider time, but you know I would just like to hold you in My Radiance until every one of you just dissolve those outer garments of imperfection, and then We go on together. That is the way the atmosphere in the room is tonight. It is so beautiful that in a moment's stillness the very outer atmosphere throbs with the Joy of Freedom which It is, that Joy of Freedom which is yours NOW. Will you not accept It in Its fullness? Oh, just think—

that Freedom which encompasses all Perfection! Stand eternally glorified in Its Radiance forever!

Tonight I offer the Eternal Blessings of the Great Host of Ascended Masters, the Legion of Light, the Great Cosmic Beings, the Gods of the Mountains, the Angelic Host, and My own Love to enfold you with Its Courage, Strength, and Conscious Dominion; to sustain you and quickly lift you unto Our Freedom from every limitation and discord of every kind, until you too, like this Good Brother, can say to all limiting appearances of discord, "You have no power!" Then they have no power in your world. Oh, if you could feel that! I know you can! You can feel it—now! Say to all limiting appearances or discord of any kind: "You have no power! 'Mighty I AM Presence,' take command of my world! Fill it with Your Perfection, and hold Your Dominion within it forever!" Then feel the Glory of It actually operating.

The Blessings of the Great Cosmic Light enfold each one of you unto your Perfection and Ascension. My Love enfolds you forever in Its Transcendent Light.

CHA ARA'S DISCOURSE

RATANA'S 100% GROUP — ALHAMBRA, CALIFORNIA

MARCH 19, 1937

HOW fortunate, oh, Beloved Ones of the Light, that you have entered into this Great Stream which is endless in Its onward Journey into your Perfection. We, who have gone the way and know the requirements of all mankind, stand by, always waiting the opportunity to give all possible Assistance at this time, in cooperation with the Great Cosmic Law.

Think of the privilege you have today in this Understanding of the Light — in being the Light, in calling the Light into action, in calling your Mighty Tube of Light into action from the "Mighty I AM Presence," to hold Its Invincible Protection about you!

How did We attain Our Freedom? By that very identical Activity: First, by the Acknowledgment of Our Mighty God Presence, the "Mighty I AM." Second, by calling It into action to produce that Mighty Tube of Light, Invisible to all human discord and creation. Then, We were able to hold Ourselves in the Balance between the human and the Divine, to allow Our Mighty "Presence" to pour Its Mighty Intelligent Energy through Our Bodies, out through

75

the Heart, into Our worlds, and have the Perfection which It is.

Beloved Ones, only Those who have gone the way that all mankind must go into the Ascension, know what your requirement is. The one who has not yet attained cannot possibly know. Therefore, your only Intelligent Information must come from Those who have made the Journey just a little ahead of you. We have made that Journey and therefore are able to give you Assistance, as yet little understood. Even the greatest of your Heart's comprehension of the Assistance which is at hand is little, in comparison with what you will ere long understand.

Please be aware of this, for only as you progress by holding your attention to your "Mighty I AM Presence" and the Great Host of Ascended Masters, will you steadily and surely Ascend, Ascend, and Ascend, until you pass the Balance of the human into the Divine. Then will you suddenly become aware of a clearness, an alertness, and fullness of the Power of your "Presence" within you and your world. Then will your Decree—then will your Call to the "Presence" be answered instantly.

With Ourselves, no longer is there anything within Our Consciousness or World that causes an effect of anything but Perfection. Therefore, when We call to the "Presence," instantly it is done. If We require something through a precipitated activity, it is there.

The world of substance obeys Us in whatever octave it may be. In your octave of human experience, the substance is necessarily very dense; but as you Ascend from one octave into another, the substance becomes more pliable, more easily brought into the form which you decree. Therefore with Us, We have but to feel, express the Desire, and It is there in manifested form. You are rapidly approaching the time when you can extend your hand and receive the manifestation.

Only as human doubts and fears have caused mankind, yourselves included, to limit the Power of the Life which beats your Heart to express more fully, are you yet unable to call and have it answered instantly. Yet among the Students all over America there are those who are being answered almost instantly. The Messenger before you, has come to find that he can call and it is answered, he can decree and it is fulfilled almost instantly. So today We want to convey this Truth to you—into your feeling world. Tonight, while I speak to you, there will come forth into your feeling world the Truth which I speak to you, through the Power of Radiation. It will hold Its Anchorage within your feeling world, to render you the Service required.

I know it is not easy for the human to realize the Simplicity, the Power with which these Great Laws cause manifestation, or how you may manipulate this substance about you and fulfill the requirement, which is your need today or in the future. Therefore, as you continue to decree for greater and greater Perfection to fill your world, through the momentum there gathers tremendous speed; and you not only gain in confidence, but in your activity. Therefore you will find as you go forth in your Application, each time it acts more quickly. But watch out, Dear Hearts, that you do not try to make your Application until you have reminded yourselves that when you call your "Presence" into Action, It knows no resistance or interference — but It proceeds with the Power of the Universe to fulfill your requirements!

This is so imperative for you to keep before the outer consciousness. Then your Application will act with tremendously greater speed, because the human, through momentum and that which is within your feeling world of which you are unaware, will many times seemingly obstruct your way, until you learn that it is necessary to remind the outer intellect that no human creation is an obstruction in the way, when you call forth the Energy from the "Presence," into you, through you, and out into your world.

Now then, you may call your "Presence" to project forth a Ray of Light, and the "Presence" fulfills the condition for that Service; but for your Victory, through yourself must come the Radiance which will one day set you free. You can give great Service even now, by calling your "Presence" to project the Rays of Light and send the Energy forth to perform the Service of the Light; but for you to gain the Victory, remember It must come through the purifying of your human form, in order for you to have your Eternal Victory.

After these two years of close association with you, do you realize how close has become that association? Perhaps you do not see Us; but does that prove that We are not moving about among you? Not at all. Remind your outer intellect that many of the things you are using in your outer world you do not see; yet you accept them, do you not? Just tonight, when you heard the Broadcast you did not see the speaker; you did not see the lines or wires connecting you with that which produced the action, did you? Yet you heard it; you received its blessing and it was quite natural to you. Why cannot mankind receive the Reality, the Blessing of the Great Host of Ascended Masters, as readily as they receive the blessing of your radio, or the use of the airplane whose propeller becomes invisible in its power to carry you foward? Yet it is there acting.

Therefore, Dear Ones, with your attention called to these various Activities which are blessing you, but yet invisible, you will see how practical is this Understanding of the Ascended Masters. They alone represent the Perfection of the "Mighty I AM Presence."

One day you will become as We are. It is not a matter of can you, but you have to! Understand that please, will you not? It is not a matter of your choice. One day, you are compelled to enter Our World, the Octave of the Ascended Masters. Your acceptance today of this Instruction and full Power of the "Mighty I AM Presence," will enable that to come about with a speed which will cut off many embodiments.

Do you realize, oh, Precious Ones, that in this Understanding of your "Mighty I AM Presence" and the Blessing which the Ascended Masters, the Legion of Light, and the Great Cosmic Beings offer you, with earnest attention to your "Presence," you can acquire in this embodiment what might take many? Remember, Precious Ones, when your attention is earnestly given to your "Presence," that instant your Ascension has begun! Do not let the human, your own or anyone else's, be foolish enough to say to you, "That cannot be." I tell you it is! And who should know better than We who have gone the Way?

Now then, if the human intellect is too arrogant to believe the Law of which We are the Fulfillment, then We cannot assist; but those who will believe the Truths We speak to them, because We are actually the Fulfillment of those Truths—then We can be of almost limitless Assistance to them. This is what We are offering the precious Children of the Light who have been drawn under the Radiation of Our Beloved Saint Germain.

You know, it is said that I resemble Saint Germain. Well, I feel quite honored. Remember, oh, People of America! Saint Germain is the One who has enabled this Freedom to come to you! No other One of the Ascended Masters, Dear Hearts, came forth, stood His ground, and fulfilled that which He declared was and could be. He has proved that He knew whereof He spoke.

Today, a great number of your blessed people of America are proving for themselves the Great Truths which He uttered. He has worked, has labored, for more than two hundred years for your Beloved America, My Beloved America. Do you not think that We love America as well as you? Knowing that America must be the Cup that carries the Light that lights the World, do you not think We should love your America as only those who see with Unlimited Vision can love?

While I give you Beloved Ones great credit for your ability to love, Our Ability far transcends yours. Does that sound strange to you? Not at all. Only as you become free in the Light, do you realize how fragmentary is your ability to release the unlimited Power of Divine Love to bless everywhere. As this Good Messenger has told you, when Saint Germain, for his Instruction, released that great flood of Love in his presence, he knew that he had never known what real Love was before. So it will be with you, as you Ascend, and Ascend, and Ascend—higher and higher—into the Consciousness and Activity of your "Presence." Then, too, will you understand that in your greatest outpouring to those on Earth you love, it is but a fragmentary part of that with which you will flood the World in the greater Understanding and Acceptance of your "Mighty I AM Presence."

Mankind should not feel that they have to be with each other in physical form to pour forth that great Love. As these two Beloved Messengers have come to know, their Love for each other is perhaps twenty times greater than it was before they entered into this Great Stream of Light and Activity. Yet sometimes for days they scarcely see each other in the Service they are rendering. So We want you to know, Dear Hearts, there is no absence in the Presence and Power of Divine Love. Whether you are held within each other's embrace, or whether you are miles apart, it makes no difference; and should not make any difference in the outpouring of your love and the loyalty of that love to each other.

We rejoice exceedingly in the privilege that We have, to be of Assistance, oh, Beloved Ones. Your precious Hearts are reaching out so intensely, not only for Freedom, but for your Ascension. Just think what has been accomplished in so short a time—a little more than two years! Oh, Precious Ones here in California, in a little more than one year you have gained within your Precious Hearts that wondrous conviction, feeling, and desire for the Ascension, which it is possible for you to attain.

Think of it! People who have been in this Understanding of the "I AM" for only one year, before coming into It, could not have even conceived such a thing was possible. Yet today thousands and thousands have accepted, in the fullness of their feeling, the Reality of their Ascension, and are working toward It with all earnestness.

As you have been told before, Precious Hearts, if for any reason you do not accomplish your Ascension in this embodiment—in your understanding, Application, and powerful reaching forth for It, you would be certain to make It in the next embodiment. Remember, you carry with you everything of the achievement you have attained so far. Now, with the use of the Violet Consuming Flame, you can dissolve all discordant creations about you. Then when you return again, you have nothing to meet here but the Glory and Perfection which the Understanding of this "Presence" holds for you. Its Perfection waits to meet you. Then instead of your human creation, the Blazing Light meets you here; you go forth quickly in that Blazing Light, into your Ascension in the next embodiment.

Pardon Me if I talk too rapidly. We rejoice today in the Glory that is yours and in the great Expansion of the Light within your precious Hearts. We see It, Dear Ones, oh, as clearly as you see the faces of each other. We see and know your achievement. This is why in these wondrous days, We utilize every opportunity to convey to you Words of encouragement. Not only do those Words go forth, but Our Radiation pours out through those Words and acts within your feeling world, although you may not yet comprehend much of it. The Light is acting there just as surely as I am telling you. In Our Radiance, even now, many of you feel Its Glory within your Heart — the warmth and Radiance of the Divine Love from your "Presence." Even as I call It forth, the chest area of the Messenger is almost glowing enough for you to see it physically, and that Light is acting within you. In your 100% Groups, I say this to you tonight: A Great Service is being rendered America and the World, but do you know that something else is being done for you individually? Just for a moment *feel* this deeply! We are trying in many ways to bring your 100% Groups to a certain achievement. This is why you were impelled to start them. We want to bring you to a point where We can show you the Manifestation of these Inner Powers, which will enlighten all tremendously who are prepared for it.

This Good Messenger has had to receive certain

Preparation. Each One who dictates must have that One's own Radiance established within and about him, to enable Us to flash these Words before him which he conveys to you. This has now become such a natural activity. There is only a breath between Our Visibility and the Radiance which went forth from his shoulders to the waist tonight, in this Light which I have called forth into action within you. As the 100% Groups are more and more prepared for it, who knows when some very delightful, beautiful thing will suddenly show you all the proof you want of that which the Messengers have so earnestly endeavored to convey to you?

This is not an imaginary thing. We are not imaginary Beings. As the Great Divine Director said last night, We are really more Real than you are. Perfection is Real, more Real than that which contains imperfection, is it not? Therefore, We are the Reality.

Oh, Beloved Ones, it is such a beautiful thing to come into this closeness with you, wherein We can reach into your Heart and feeling world and give the Assistance that you so much crave. All mankind must have this until they come to a certain point of Self-mastery. As you understand this, deeper and deeper gratitude comes forth. Then you prepare the way more and more, not only for the greater flood from your "Presence," but for that which We can give to you.

We love to hold your hands, and sometimes We move about you when you least expect it. From anywhere We are, We need but to direct Our Attention to you to see what is required. When you give your attention to Us—your "Presence" first and then to Us—your Radiance, your Ray of Light comes to Us like an arrow. We know it and come back on your Ray of Light with all that is required or permitted.

Do you not see, oh, Beloved Ones, how practical is all of this Mighty Activity? Now, while I am speaking these Words, try to accept the Feeling of how practical is every particle of this so-called Transcendent Activity. It is Transcendent from the human sense, but it is all so practical and natural! The Activity of the Ascended Masters is the most practical thing in the world. As you come to feel that, you will enable Us to do so much more for you. Then, so much greater Assistance can be given than if you felt It was something too Transcendent for you yet to reach. Mankind has gone on throughout the centuries since the time of Jesus and His Ministry, feeling He was a Being so far beyond them that He could not be reached. His Heart has ached so many times for mankind when He wanted to come close and give Assistance, yet the very feeling of individuals held Him away at a great distance.

Once you learn the power of your feeling world, what a transformation will take place in your Life.

Hold your feeling harmonious to the Great "Presence." Call It with great determination into action to produce Its Perfection and hold Its Dominion in your world. Oh, then the Joy, the Beauty, the Freedom, and the Happiness that is yours! Oh, Dear Hearts, you do not need longer remain in unhappiness of any kind. Oh, do not let the human any longer have dominion to make you unhappy.

The Great Light which gives you Life and beats your Heart is Free, oh, so Free! Yet the ignorance of the human tries to bind that Light and to say to that which the Light produces: "You are mine! You must obey me!" What nonsense! Oh, the Freedom of the Light to give every human being Freedom! Once mankind learns to do that, then very great will be the happiness mankind will experience.

Is it not a tragedy, Dear Hearts, when human beings, for any reason whatsoever, try to bind others to them? It is not the Law of Life. Freedom is the Law of Life. That does not mean license to do wrong things, not by any means! But it does mean in the feeling world each one should let every other one be perfectly free. Just call their "Mighty I AM Presence" into action and feel it. Then all must be in perfect, harmonious accord. This does not mean that men and women should go out and pick up with each other's wives and husbands or anything of the kind. That is not freedom! It is worse bondage than ever, because when mankind sets up causes, God alone knows how far-reaching are the effects. Freedom means, in your feeling world, to let everyone feel the full Glory of his own "Presence." Wonderful! wonderful! wonderful indeed! Only We who have attained that Freedom know just how wonderful It is.

Tonight I wish to remind you how very wonderful is the adoration in your songs to these Great Ones. Oh, it is very wonderful! That harmony and rhythm of your love and adoration pouring forth to Them in song, enables Them to come back to you in a Transcendent Manner which words could not describe. Tonight you sang so wonderfully, really. You know there are two kinds of singing: one that sings from the intellect and the other that sings from the Heart. You have heard singers who were as cold as ice, haven't you? Then, you have heard those whose very Radiance glows with the loving Kindness of the Wondrous "Presence" and Activity within them. Those sing from the Heart. You, tonight, sang from the Heart. You know the poetical phrase, "Two hearts that beat as one." It is far more than that—many Hearts are beating as one tonight.

Oh, Dear Ones, do you not see how, in the Acknowledgment of the Great, the Mighty "Presence," all the world becomes an expression of Divine Love? All the world becomes lovers—expressing Divine Love. Do you not see how wonderful it is? These Beloved

Messengers have learned to do that—to pour forth such a Power of Divine Love to the Students that It gives them happiness they never knew existed before in their love to each other. Their love before was very great, and yet it was not a fragment in comparison to this Great Love of the "Mighty I AM Presence" which pours forth to flood the world of the Students everywhere.

Oh, Precious Ones, you have entered into a World of Light, Love, Freedom, and Perfection. Accept it unto its fullness in all activity of you and your world. Remember, Dear Ones, no longer need you accept or hold within you the slightest inharmony in your bodies; for you know now the Light in your Heart, your physical Heart in your body, is your "Mighty I AM Presence" acting there. I leave this Statement with you tonight. Remember, your Heart is your "Mighty I AM Presence" acting within your human form. Therefore, Its Radiance pouring forth in every cell of your body through the Threads of Light that come forth, and the Points of Light within those cells, enables you to be a dynamo of the Energy from your Heart. Then to think that mankind should ever have thought anyone could have Heart trouble! It is never the Heart that is troubled, Dear Hearts; it is your feeling, just your feeling that is troubled—not the Heart.

So remember, remind yourselves, oh, Precious

Ones, that your Heart here, giving Life to your body and circulation through it, is your "Mighty I AM Presence" in your human form. Do you not see then, how you cannot help but feel the closeness, the Reality of your "Mighty I AM Presence" within you, producing Its Perfection instantly at your Command? At your Command, a great intensified Activity must sweep out all imperfection of every kind.

Many times this Good Messenger has been brought to those who were so ill and weak that they could not walk, and after twenty minutes got up and walked with full strength—showing that the trouble which was thought to be the Heart was only a human concept in the feeling world of that individual. As soon as that was removed from the feeling world, the strength of the "Presence" was there.

Oh, do not limit yourselves again in any manner whatsoever, Precious Ones. I plead with you. Your "Mighty I AM Presence" is your Storehouse of Health, Strength, Supply, Money, Happiness, Joy—everything you require is here. The Fullness of It is anchored there [above in the Electronic Body]! It is ready to pour forth, without limit, everything you require! Will you not accept that? So far as your money supply is concerned, will you not accept your "Presence" as your Storehouse? Then, if channels are necessary for your supply, those channels must work in harmony for your supply. Do you not see how it cannot fail?

If any of you are lacking for your money supply in any way, it is because in your feeling world there is the consciousness of your limitation. In the intellect you are not aware of this obstruction acting in your feeling. Then say: " 'Mighty I AM Presence,' take out of me the feeling that is obstructing the way! You release Your Supply of money I require in the Service of the Light!"

Oh, Precious Ones, do you not see it could not fail, not for one moment? We want you to become fully conscious that your "Presence" holds ready to pour forth at any given moment everything that you require for your happiness and comfort. After all, it is through your joy and happiness that the release comes quickly of everything your "Presence" holds for you. As you stand before the Chart of your "Presence" each day, feel Its Joy and Happiness surging forth, and filling your world and home. It will do it so much more powerfully than anything mankind has yet conceived through the human activity.

Tonight, oh, Beloved Ones, you shall go forth carrying My Joy, My Happiness, My Consciousness of your supply of every good thing which you require for use. It shall remain active there within your feeling world. I so decree it. Will you not accept this in its fullness for your Freedom? How do I know that which I desire to anchor within your feeling world for your use is acting there? By the Activity of the Light within you. Even as I issued that Decree, this moment the Light expands within you in response to My great Desire to help you. That is how We know whether Our Decree or Desire for your Assistance is acting or not. I am grateful that you are able to accept My Humble Service which I have offered.

In the fullness of the Great Light, "the Light of the World," I call Its Activity to hold you in Its Wondrous Embrace, raising, raising, raising you, until that moment when you suddenly feel yourself wholly free from every limitation, and you call forth through your greater Understanding this Blessing for all mankind.

Do you realize, oh, Beloved Ones, tonight in this hour We have been in a Heavenly, Eternal Sanctuary of the Light? It will always continue to expand for you. My Love enfolds you forever, and may your acceptance make it ever more and more possible for Our Assistance to come to you. I thank you.

LADY MASTER NADA'S DISCOURSE

"I AM" SCHOOL — LOS ANGELES, CALIFORNIA

MARCH 20, 1937

BELOVED Children of the Light, of the "Mighty I AM Presence," My Joy is boundless tonight in pouring forth to you from My Heart, My Love, Courage, Strength, and Activity, which shall always continue to act within your feeling world.

You perhaps understand that besides this physical body which you have, you have what is termed an emotional body, or a feeling body, outside of your physical body and penetrating it. Your feeling body is your Powerhouse, or the means by which you are supplied with energy which acts through your physical body. Now then, as you understand this and your "Mighty I AM Presence," you will find you can call your "Presence" forth to charge your minds and bodies with all the energy and strength that you require; you can call forth all the courage you need.

Call the "Presence" to give you confidence in yourself to apply the Law of your "Presence," which is your Life. As you continue to call your "Presence" into action, you will find each day you gain a greater confidence — not only that your "Presence" is there and does answer you, but you have a feeling of greater calmness

93

and peace within yourself through calling your "Presence" into action.

Having had long, long experience with the children of Earth, it is always My Great Joy to be of Service whenever the opportunity affords. The children of Los Angeles have responded so wonderfully to the Instruction which Saint Germain has brought forth. Now, We shall do everything We can to make the children of Los Angeles an outstanding pattern, an example. Now notice! You are to be an example for children everywhere, because your city is one where children from all over America come to visit. You know that, and therefore, as Children of the "Mighty I AM Presence," you will be the example for your visiting friends who come here, will you not? You know that is considerable responsibility; for you want to be a shining Light and example, not only to the grown-up people, but to the visiting friends who will come here. I tell you that in the next two years many, many from various parts of the United States will come here to visit you. You see!

Therefore, you want to be so alert, so attentive to your Understanding of the "Presence" by applying It in all your schoolwork, that when your visiting friends come, you can with full confidence stand before the Chart and explain It to them just as this Good Messenger does. Will each one of you just feel a great earnest desire to become so familiar with the

Explanation of the Chart, that you can quickly and readily explain It, any instant you might be called upon to do so? It is a very wonderful thing, Dear Children. Do you realize, Precious Ones, that children for thousands of years have not had this privilege before?

This Understanding of the "Mighty I AM Presence," which Saint Germain has brought forth, has not been in the outer world for thousands of years. That is a long time from the human standpoint, but it is true. Now that you have this privilege in the Understanding of your "Mighty I AM Presence," It does make everything easy for you. It helps you to maintain self-control, dominion of your feelings! It enables the Power from your "Presence" to flood forth to do the things you require.

As you go forth in this Understanding, you will find as the energy continues to flood forth through you, that It gains what We term "momentum." I mean, through the continuous use of a thing, you gain power by it. That is what We mean by momentum. Often you will find where there is a requirement, that your "Presence" will suddenly charge Its Currents of Energy through to bless you—even sometimes before you ask. This is what We want you to feel, Dear Ones: that after you have called the "Presence" into action for a while, It begins to act ofttimes even before you call. Then you will find that your "Presence," through the Higher Mental Body, is always standing on guard through you and for you. Do not forget that in your homes you can render such a beautiful Service to your brothers, sisters, friends, father, and mother. Every night will you do this for Me? Before you go to sleep, will you take a copy of the Chart, either in the Books, Magazine, or some copy of the Chart, and speaking to your "Mighty I AM Presence," simply say: " 'Mighty I AM Presence,' now You hold my body, while it sleeps, in Your Wondrous Embrace of Light. When I awaken in the morning, You take charge of my mind and body! Cause me to do the Perfect Thing always which I should do to produce the greatest happiness for myself and those about me, and to produce the greatest success in all I desire to do." Remember, you are the one who must call the "Presence" into action to govern your world. Do you know that your world is just that which extends around you for, say, the distance across this room — this part of the room here from the door forward — about twenty feet in a circle; that would be the world of the average individual. Now notice this closely! If this were a complete circle, it would be what the average person's world consists of. Does that seem a small world? Well you would be surprised how much is contained within that world!

Then your part, your objective, or that which you

require, is to call your "Presence" into action to not only control your mind and body, but this world which extends around you. It means to a large extent your feeling world and that which you have created.

Now, Blessed Children, I wish to give this to you because it means so much. You see on the Chart the Violet Consuming Flame. Call your "Presence" to pass It from your feet up and consume every discordant thing which you have ever created through the centuries, because you have lived many times besides this lifetime—in similar bodies. If you will call the "Presence" to use the Violet Consuming Flame, you will have very little difficulty in keeping your feelings harmonized; and that is what all mankind requires today.

The conditions which exist about humanity through so much inharmony make it difficult for the average person to control himself and keep harmonious, but it can be done easily in the Knowledge of your "Presence." Then, you can realize the need of the Tube of Light about you, as you see there on the Chart.

How many of you try to call the "Presence" into action and form this Tube of Light about you? How many of you do that? *(many hands go up)* Well that is lovely. There are three things that are so important to you: first, to know your "Presence" is the Giver of all Life to you and to the World; second, to call the "Presence" to use the Violet Consuming Flame and take out of this world of yours every discordant thing and accumulation of wrongly qualified energy.

Remember now, you are living in a circle of your own world! As you call the "Presence" to pass the Violet Consuming Flame through you, It is just within and around your body. As you call the "Presence" to send the Violet Consuming Flame from your feet up, and also consume that which is around you (and will you blessed grown-ups take note of this as well), everything out here which would be discordant in this circle of your world is drawn in and consumed by that use of the Violet Consuming Flame. Every discordant thing that you have ever generated or created will be drawn into the Flame, dissolved, and consumed. It is a very wonderful thing, Precious Ones.

As you understand and, in the Knowledge of your "Presence," do this, you will free your world from everything which has disturbed you up to the present time. Then when you call the "Presence" into action, you will find a much more powerful Activity of your "Presence" than if It had to pour Its Energy through the discordant creation which is there. Humanly with your physical body you cannot do that; but when you call your "Presence" into action to do it, It acts whether you see It or not, for that is not necessary.

The third thing is calling your "Presence" to form about you this Tube of Light, as you see It on the Chart. Then, you can move in the world untouched by the discord of human creation in the outer world, which you must necessarily meet. If you draw such a Tube of Light about you, do you not see that the other people who come near you will feel the peaceful Radiance from the "Presence" pouring forth from the Tube of Light, and they would not desire to be discordant?

As you come to understand these simple things and wonderful activities, you will find your "Presence" will govern your world with such joyous, happy Freedom as you have never been able to maintain, until you began to experience it through calling your "Presence" into action.

You see, while it is true the "Presence" supplies Life to your body sufficiently so you can move about, yet that is not enough. The "Presence" waits and has waited a long, long time for mankind to understand the "Presence" is there and that the individual must make the Call to It, to enable It to release a greater volume of energy—a greater quantity of energy—to flow in and through your body and out into your world through your Heart.

The first part of your physical body which is formed is your Heart; and that is where your "Presence," through Its Ray of Light and Energy, is anchored — within your Heart, within your body. This is how God is within, and God is without — the "Mighty I AM Presence." Only a very small part of God is within the Heart, until you consciously know the "Presence" is there. It is very small and simply supplies the ordinary use of Life to sustain the physical body.

When you know the "Presence" is there, you can call It into action. As you practice It, you continue to call forth a greater and greater volume or quantity of the Energy from your "Presence" to produce Its Perfection in your home, world, schoolroom, or wherever it is. Will you not do this for Me?

Just before you come into your schoolroom each day, will you call your "Mighty I AM Presence" into action to charge the schoolroom with this Mighty Perfection and Understanding, so when you enter into your schoolwork, all will quickly grasp what is said and be able to apply it successfully in your studies? You will find such joy if you will do that, and I will help you. Would you like Me to help you? I will be glad to if you will do as I ask and keep such great harmony in your schoolroom, such great love, and such great joy. Then the harmony makes it easy for your "Mighty I AM Presence" to give you Its Comprehension and Understanding in your studies, or in whatever is required for you to do during the day. As you do this, you will find such a joy filling your mind, body, and world, such a happiness filling your schoolroom, that you will just love to come and enjoy it so much while you are here. You will feel that great loving desire to bless each other in all you do.

Sometimes, you know, you have studied awhile; and all of a sudden you straighten up and rest, as it were, for a few moments. In that moment, you can call forth the Blessing of the "Mighty I AM Presence" for each one in the room; and do you know what that will mean to you? Suppose there are a dozen students in the room. If you will call the Blessing on the other eleven, then you get eleven times the power of your Blessing upon yourself which you call forth for the others. Do you understand that? When you call the Blessing upon eleven other people, you get eleven times for yourself the Blessing which you call upon the others. Is that not worthwhile? It is very wonderful as you come to understand it.

Tonight while I am talking to you, I am pouring forth into your feeling world those Qualities which will become active within you, which I see you need. Can and will you remember that at any time you need extra Assistance, first send your thought, your feeling, your Call, to your "Mighty I AM Presence"; then if you wish to call to Nada, you will always have My Answer come back to you. As you try that out for a while and you find the response coming more tangible each time, then such a great joy will fill your Heart; for you know you have a Friend to whom you can call and always get the Help.

In your home, if the need gets very great, call to your "Presence" first, then call to Me; and I shall always come back on a Ray of Light to you, to give the Help that you might need for yourself, in your home or your activity. As you do that, you will find a Great Peace and Joy always abiding within you.

Tonight as I spread My Mantle of Pink over you, which I have done while I have been talking, you absorb It into your bodies, for It is Self-luminous, Intelligent Substance. This means that It is Light-Substance — L I G H T — Light-Substance, which you are absorbing. It is the Ascended Masters' Substance, which the human cannot qualify or clothe with any discordant feeling. In that way, I shall be able to give you Assistance, in your cooperation with Me, to do many things that are very wonderful.

How many of you here are interested in art? (*many hands go up*) Oh, wonderful! Do you know that those little hands which you hold up are the Hands of your "Mighty I AM Presence"? Do you know it is true and it is right? Your hands are the Hands of the "Mighty I AM Presence." Then if you want to do some work in art, you simply say: " 'Mighty I AM Presence,' now You take charge of my hands! Cause me to do perfect drawing, to produce perfect designs or pictures," or whatever it is you wish to do; " 'Mighty I AM Presence,' You take charge of these hands! Cause me to produce the most beautiful things, even more beautiful than I can imagine from the human stand-point." As you do that and keep calling the "Presence" to do it, you will find you will be producing the most beautiful things in pictures, designs of flowers, or whatever it is.

How many are interested in music, either instru-mental or voice? (*many hands go up*) Splendid! Then, Dear Children, remember that your voice, your vocal cords by which you sing, are those of the "Mighty I AM Presence," and you simply say: "Now 'Mighty I AM Presence,' my throat is Your Throat! My voice is Your Voice. Therefore, You sing perfectly through my voice." If you will do that, you will be astonished how wonderfully and quickly you will begin to sing beautifully and perfectly.

You see, it is so in every activity of your phys-ical body in the outer world. For instance: suppose you wanted your body to become beautiful and perfect. If it is not as beautiful as you want it to be, simply say: " 'Mighty I AM Presence,' take charge of my mind and body! Pour Your Mighty Currents of Energy through me with such intensity that my body becomes as Beautiful and Perfect as You are." Or in a more simplified expression: " 'Mighty I AM Presence,' make me beautiful and perfect!" Then whatever is within your physical body that is not perfect will have to give place to that which is perfect. You see?

In these simple ways, you can call an All-powerful Action of the "Presence" into your Life to produce the Perfection which you require, or that which gives you happiness — because many times people, and children especially, find one thing or another which makes them feel disturbed or discouraged or produces something that is not desirable. Therefore, to anything that attempts to find action in your world which is not Perfection, say: " 'Mighty I AM Presence,' You take this out of my feeling world and replace it by Your Satisfaction and Perfection, Your Perfect Activity." Then, you will be able to do the things that you require quickly, easily, beautifully, and perfectly.

Now suppose you want your physical body and its action to become perfect. Say: " 'Mighty I AM Presence,' this is Your physical body. You take Perfect Command of it! Make it come into Perfect Order and Perfect Action." As you continue to do that, then your "Presence" will produce Its Perfect Symmetry of body and Perfect Action in your body which you require. Do you know, Precious Children, in this Knowledge of your "Mighty I AM Presence," you can produce in your body, through your body, and into your world whatever Perfection you wish to call forth?

Now, I am going to ask the Beloved Messengers and Mrs. Mundy if they will make copies of this which I have said to you, so that each one of the Schools can have it to read to the children whenever they feel so inclined. I shall be very grateful if they will do that; because each time it is read, I will be able to pour forth My Radiance through these Words which I have spoken to you, the same as I have spoken them tonight. That will give you a constant use of My Ascended Master Consciousness and Feeling which I am pouring forth to you tonight.

After a while, you will come to understand much more clearly than you do now, what these Words have meant to you tonight. As you keep calling it forth, then clearer and clearer will come the Understanding of that which I have anchored within your feeling world tonight to give you the Assistance.

I want you to know how great are My Joy and Love in this little talk to you, but I do not want to hold you longer tonight. Just remember — Nada was with you in person tonight and dictated these Words to you, because of My Great Love for you. Will you remember that and feel it is a part of your body and your Life and your activity always? This will give Me the greatest opportunity to give you all the Assistance that I can. Unless I can have your attention upon Me, I cannot do so much for you.

Do you remember, sometimes when you have seen

the man who sells balloons, how those little balloons are fastened to strings? You have seen him hold ever so many in his hand by the strings. In the same way there are threads of Light that go out from Me to you tonight, by which I give you those Qualities which I want to convey into your feeling world. This is the way I am pouring out tonight, just like Threads of Light — oh, through little tiny Rays that go out. Will you sometimes remember that — how it was done this night? Then you will have tremendous Assistance and Blessings.

I give you the Blessing of Saint Germain, Jesus, the Great Divine Director, and the Great Host of Ascended Masters. They want so much to assist the Children of Earth to their Freedom and the Understanding of the Great Source of all Life, the "Mighty I AM Presence," which every human being on Earth is seeking, but many do not yet know it in the physical senses. All will one day come to know it, for the Work which Saint Germain has brought forth is spreading so rapidly throughout mankind and the World! One day all mankind will again come to know this "Mighty I AM Presence" and have the Blessing which It alone can give, and the Happiness which It can produce.

Now, there is one more thing I want to say before We stop and it is concerning the money you require in your world now and in the future. So long as that is the means of exchange, remember, Dear Children, now is the time for you to anchor this firmly within your consciousness: Your "Mighty I AM Presence," which supplies Life to your body, is also the Treasure House. I mean by that, It is the Intelligence that opens the way and gives the supply of money to you which you require for things in the outer world. There are many grown-ups who do not quite understand this; but nevertheless, you as children today can understand that your "Mighty I AM Presence" is your Treasure House—the means by which your supply of money comes to you.

If you will always call to your "Mighty I AM Presence" to open the way and see that you are always supplied with the money you require in your Service of the Light, then the "Presence" will provide ways and means through the Power of Divine Love and Order, so you can and will always have the supply of money you require for the things you wish to use in your outer physical activity.

This is the reason why I am asking Mrs. Mundy and the Messengers to see that corrected copies of this are given to whoever conducts the School—not copies to be given out, but just to be read to the students whenever they feel impelled to do it, because this will carry the Radiation to you each time.

Now in the Blessing of the "Mighty I AM Presence," the Great Host of Ascended Masters, the Mighty Legion of Light, and the Great Cosmic Beings, I ask the Great Cosmic Light to hold you enveloped in Its Mighty Radiance, to produce perfect physical bodies; clean, pure, alert minds; and firm, determined attention to your "Mighty I AM Presence," which will enable you to have the fullest Release from your "Presence," the most powerful Activity possible. Your gratitude should always pour out to your "I AM Presence" for everything that is given to you for use in your Life.

I thank you, Precious Children, for this wondrous attention which you have given to Me, and your reward shall be great in return for it. You Precious Children! Do you realize that you have given just as perfect attention as any class of grown-up people? That is a very wonderful thing. You know how sometimes children wiggle around and get restless? Well, you did not, and this has been quite a long time that I have been talking to you.

So I just rejoice to see how you have already gained in your Understanding of your "Presence." It proves to Me that you must have a very lovely teacher who is teaching you in this Work. Do you love your teacher very much? Do all of you? (*Many answer "Yes."*) Fine!

Now just remember that My Love enfolds each one of you always, unto your Perfection and your Ascension—just as I have Myself and as all the Ascended Masters have made Their Ascension. All make It in the same way. Your Goal is not only to perfect yourself, but to Ascend eventually into this Electronic Body—your "Mighty I AM Presence"—when you become an Ascended Being, the same as I am today, as Saint Germain, the same as Jesus and the Divine Director. So you see your Goal is twofold: to free yourself from limitations which the human has created and then make your Ascension. That will all come; and those who understand the "Mighty I AM Presence" in this embodiment, if they do not accomplish the Ascension now, then in the next embodiment they will, with very great certainty. This is My Love and My Wish which I have conveyed to you tonight. I trust it may be read to you so you will be reminded sometimes of this night, in which We lived in a World not made with hands.

In the atmosphere of this room tonight is the Radiance of your "Mighty I AM Presence," amplified by the Great Host of Ascended Masters. It has become a new World while We are here. You have entered into that new World which will continue to act within and about you the rest of your earthly pilgrimage here. Will you just always feel that?

My Love enfolds you forever in Its Transcendent Light. I hold you close in My Embrace of Love forever, unto your Victory and Ascension. I thank you.

ARCTURUS' DISCOURSE

LANNING'S GROUP — LOS ANGELES, CALIFORNIA

MARCH 21, 1937

— MORNING —

GREAT loving Hearts of America! Today it is My Privilege to draw your attention to Activities near at hand, in which you are a very important part. As you have been informed, on the seventh of April there will come a Great Cosmic Onrush of Light into the Earth.

Today I come to you to give Assistance; for while you are hearing My Words, My Light shall go forth into the mental and feeling world of mankind, to prepare all everywhere for the Onrush of this Great Cosmic Light. You may see some Manifestation of It or you may not, depending upon the Wisdom of the Great Cosmic Beings who are sending It forth; but there will be those of the "I AM" Students who will feel the great Exhilaration, the great Uplift that day. Those who do feel It, and even those who do not, will you qualify that eternally sustained in all activity of your life henceforth?

You see, Beloved Ones, it is not only a momentary achievement. In your conscious feeling and ability, every step, every achievement acquired, you can

110

qualify to be eternally sustained and all-powerfully active forever — in your Life, your mind, body, home, world, or in whatever it is for which you require that activity.

This is such a definite, such a powerful Activity into which you have entered. This Great Stream of Life into which you have entered, may I remind you again, is Self-luminous, Intelligent Substance. Try to get the fullness of this idea. Notice! Feel within your being that you are constantly, through your acceptance of the "Presence," absorbing into the atomic structure of your body this Self-luminous, Intelligent Substance. Do you not see, Precious Ones, that you must have perfect health? You must have energy without limit to send you forth like a rocket into any achievement in any direction for Perfection!

I assure you, Precious Ones, We are entering into a dynamic activity — not as you know it, but in the calm intensity of your feeling world — We are entering into the Activity of your Freedom. It shall become manifest in your mind, body, home, world, and affairs. You are not wavering any longer, you know. Now, you straighten your spines and stand firm in the acceptance of your "Presence." Remember again, Dear Ones, your determination is the activity of the Inner Will of the "Mighty I AM Presence."

Be *determined* that America shall be free! Be *determined* that your Application brings results immediately! Do not let your human or anyone else's qualify anything that you do or call for, with anything but Instantaneous Activity! Then as you gain the momentum, you will find more and more there will come, just like rhythmic tapping, the steady acquirement of the Full Power in your Application for any achievement.

You are no longer children. You are Gods of Light in the Acknowledgment of your "Presence"! As you dissolve the cause and hold the rest of your human self that still remains, in abeyance, then your "Mighty I AM Presence" becomes the only Power acting.

During your Decrees, I stood here listening and rejoicing at the willingness of the Children of God to stand for their home—America. When you speak those Words—"The 'I AM' Country," "The Land of 'the Light of God that never fails' "—do you not realize that you have uttered the Words which release the Mightiest Power in the Universe to produce that very thing here in your America? How in the world can anything longer hold its sway of discord or deceit, when these Mighty Decrees are going forth now from nearly two hundred thousand Children of Light in America, calling with great intensity for Her Freedom? Notice the spirit with which the blessed Students of the "I AM" all over America are entering into this with a joyous exhilaration, whose Power, Dear Ones, to send forth these Mighty Decrees is doing a Work that is inconceivable. Until you reach the state of the Ascended Masters, you cannot see the Power and Light which it is producing.

No longer do the Children of America have to give way before discordant forces—whether it be in your private life, whether it be in your home, whether it be in your city or government. Say to every discordant appearance, "You have no power!" Then it does not have any power to act in your world or in your country. When you issue these Mighty Decrees for the protection of your Supreme Court, it shall be protected. The Great Cosmic Light shall sweep in on the seventh of April, bringing an added Power that will silence all deceit concerning your government! That Mighty Light shall bring America into the Power and Glory which belongs to Her. No human being or group of human beings has any power to longer charge the Earth or its atmosphere with any deception or discord. Neither have they any power to interfere with or influence the mass of mankind, to do anything that will bring discredit upon Beloved America.

Listen closely! The Call of the Children of America for this Light, for this Protection, is the only thing that has been required throughout the centuries to release and cause the Great Cosmic Light to come forth and give this Protection! You will remember in one of the Discourses I dictated, that I said: "If necessary, that Light as of Ten Thousand Suns shall sweep into the Earth and bring Relief and Protection to America," and so it shall be done! No longer is mankind helpless before these forces which individuals have not understood. Today every "I AM" Student who is in earnest understands the forces which they have to deal with, and they are fearless before them. When they call this Mighty Light into action, the Mighty Activity of the "I AM Presence," then the Power of the Universe has gone forth to do Its Perfect Work for each one, individually, collectively, and for nations.

Notice the difference, Beloved Ones, between the time when mankind did not know or accept its Divine Power, and now, when individuals have come to know this "Mighty Presence" which beats every Heart. Your Call to It actually releases a Universal Power to go forth and do that which you desire to have done. It will continue to act, unless the individual through discordant feeling obstructs the way. You alone, through inharmony, are the only one who can obstruct your way, or prevent the response to the Decree which you issue. Remember that, Beloved Ones! The whole responsibility is in your feeling world. When you issue a Decree, hold your feeling calm — determined that it shall be answered quickly. Stand by it with your determination, and it cannot fail to produce results for you.

Now the need today in America has been great. Yet see how great has been the Power released for Its Protection and Blessing. I wish, while I have the opportunity today, to bless this good brother, our Beloved Mr. Zinke, who has made possible the broadcasting of this Mighty Truth so far. I shall hold his hand in Blessing for that great kindness which he has done for America. Many, many people will be raised up to make these things possible, Dear Hearts, and their Blessing shall know no bounds.

Dear Ones, there are those in America today who, once they understand this Mighty Truth, Its Simplicity and Great Reality, will be so ready to give assistance for the freedom of mankind in America. Watch it! And please remember, Dear Ones, that no human, discordant thing has any longer any power to obstruct the way of the Light of the "Mighty I AM Presence." Anyone who tries it, is but just childish and foolish. While they will reap great unhappiness and misery through it, yet it has no power to obstruct anything in the way of the great Onrush of this Mighty Light.

Those unfortunate individuals who have viciously sought to intrude upon this Great Light are unfortunate indeed! It is very unfortunate for them. Those individuals who have sought to put forth vicious falsehood against this Beloved Messenger, God alone help them. I say to you, better had they never been born in this embodiment, than to spread falsehood against him. Watch them! You or I could not wish anything upon them which will not be theirs. The unfortunate thing is that some of mankind cannot yet understand that what they sow they must reap. Now in the Understanding of the "Mighty I AM Presence," the "I AM" Students have all Power to protect themselves. Whoever sends discord to the "I AM" Students must feel its return to act upon the sender. It seems pitiful that they do not understand.

It is the same way in America. I am drawing this picture for you that you may understand it is the same with individuals as it is with America today. Those who would practice deceit to bring in certain activities for the longer binding of America, have no power! Those individuals must reap that which they would impose upon humanity. Do you not see the Eternal Blessing which has come to mankind in the Understanding of their "Mighty I AM Presence"?

Dear Hearts, be assured you are not dealing with an uncertainty! You Beloved Students who have been so earnest and may not yet have the results you would like, I plead with you, do not be discouraged. Go on and on and on in your Mighty Application, and you cannot fail! One day you will find that wall of human creation go down. You will look through and see the Great Light which is yours. You will know then that your earnest efforts have not been in vain. No one's earnest efforts can ever be in vain in the Acknowledgment of that "Mighty I AM Presence." Today, Beloved Ones, be reassured. Go forward in your Application of the "Mighty I AM Presence." It cannot fail! And if it seems not to have produced results as quickly as you require, call the "Presence" to cleanse your feeling world of every discordant thing which may be there preventing your Application having Instantaneous Answer.

My Joy is boundless today to find before Me you who have such great strength, and whose Mighty Light will blaze forth Its Glory and give whatever Assistance is required to bring forth this Great Perfection in the World. Do not accept reports, I plead with you, Dear Ones, in the newspapers or otherwise. Do not accept any report that is less than Perfection which comes forth to your ears or your eyes. Every time a report of limitation, distress, or a disturbing thing comes, still yourself for an instant and say: " 'Mighty I AM Presence,' I refuse acceptance of that into my world or America! Take it out! Stop it forever! And do not let it occur again." You Precious Ones, if you will do that individually as you become aware of these things, oh, how quickly will they cease to act in your minds, your city, or your country.

Need I stress again to you today, how, when you issue these Decrees, they go forth into the feeling and mental world of mankind, with a Power far beyond your conception in the outer! Do not limit your Call. Just feel and know it is going forth to the very limits of America and the Universe to do its Perfect Work. The mental world of mankind is one! The feeling world of mankind is one! Do you not see how the human cannot have power to limit your activity?

Dear Hearts, from today forth, enter into the full feeling of the Power of your "Mighty I AM Presence," to go forth at your Call and do Its Perfect Work. You physically do not do that, but your Call does release the Power of the "Presence." It matters not whether your physical body is strong or so-called less strong. You blessed ladies, who represent the feeling world of the Earth, do not ever feel that you are too frail to issue these Decrees and have the most wonderful results.

Beloved Ones, may I say this to you today? We look into the atmosphere of Earth and see in the social world, which has been taught through habit to waste long hours in playing bridge and such various activities. Think, Precious Ones, what those hours spent calling forth the Perfection of the "Presence" into their own world and America would mean! Is it not curious how mankind has sought through habit— oh God!—to kill time? Think of it! Think of the millions of times that expression has been used, "Oh, I want to just kill time." Precious Ones, if you have ever uttered those words, please do not utter them again. Words are cups that carry the qualities which you express.

When We focus the Mighty Rays of Light and look upon the Earth from Our own Octave of Light, We have seen the great waste of time — human beings actually doing what their words express — "killing time." It means that you are depriving yourself of the time allotted to you here on Earth to produce Perfection in your world.

Today, Dear Ones, do not ever become weary of giving your attention to your "Presence," which can only produce Perfection in your world. I have noticed several instances among the Students of America today, since I came into the Earth's atmosphere this morning, about which I wish to warn you. I plead with you, do not let individuals who have fanatical inclinations and go off on a tangent, affect you, Dear Ones. This Good Messenger had a letter recently wherein a lady was in distress and had become a fanatic through a discarnate, because she could not call forth the Light as quickly as she wished, and she became distressed. Just because individuals who have been fanatical over all kinds of things in the past come into the "I AM" Study, and those old creations are still hanging around them, there is no reason for blaming this Glorious Presence of Light, the "Mighty I AM," for the reactions of their own mistakes of the past.

Now Dear Ones, when the Blessed Ones have understood the Instructions given, there is no excuse for those things. It is no fault of the Instruction of the "I AM." It is the fault of the human who requalifies Life's Energy, or some discarnate disturbing them.

Dear Hearts, here is one word I wish to offer you today in regard to the dismissal of discarnates. When you issue a Decree for the dismissal of a disembodied entity, do not let your feelings ever, even once again, feel that it has not been done. That is what is the matter with people who call for a discarnate to be removed. They feel it is still there. They may not know this in their outward feeling. For instance, at your Call every discarnate will be removed from within and about you. Do you realize, Precious Ones, when you call the Angels of Blue Lightning to take out of your world the discarnates, it is a Law that has to act instantly, and it cannot fail to produce results?

If the aftereffect still remains in the consciousness of the individual, then you who might see that, make the Call to the "Presence" to take out of that consciousness any remaining feeling which might be there. Then you will give great assistance to the individual who may have had a reaction to it through habit in the feeling.

Remember, in your Application there is not one

particle of it can fail, ever. While I am speaking to you, I am charging your feeling world with the Activity which gives you the Perfect Confidence, the Perfect Assurance that when you make Application, it must manifest. This is the power and certainty I want every one of you precious ones to feel, because there is no need of your going on longer when you can be free in one mighty sweep.

Just as it is with this Good Messenger—the difference between his Application ten years ago and today—it is as different as Light and darkness, because now he has gained the full confidence and power of conviction that when he issues a Decree, it is done. It must be, because he does nothing to reverse it; and you must do the same thing! Many of you are.

From today forth, the Students in southern California, and even those who are not here, are feeling this Charge into their worlds, because Our Ability is not limited to those present. Oh, that you might understand, Beloved Ones, how limitless is the Power of an Ascended Being or a Cosmic Being to act in the world of human affairs. There is no limit to the number of individuals one can reach. There is no limit to Our Power of Assistance, according to the acceptance of the individual.

Sometimes individuals who want so much to accept, still have a feeling within them that they cannot quite do it. Again you have the unbalance, shall We call it, of the intellect and the feeling. The intellect says, "I want to accept," but the feeling does not quite do it. Then say: " 'Mighty I AM Presence,' You take this resistance out of my feeling. Make it receptive to that which I want to express." Then do you see how simple is the complete regulation of your feeling world for that which you wish to have accomplished?

Do not ever admit for one second that your Application can fail. It cannot do it! Today I want to charge into your world the sure, certain, definite conviction and confidence that when you apply these Great Laws of your "Mighty I AM Presence," there is no such thing as failure possible. It cannot be! Then you will find, as in one thing after another you gain the Victory, shortly everything goes down which has limited you; and you stand forth a Being of Light and Freedom, even in the physical world of mankind.

May I call your attention today to that which you call physical? Do you know really there is no physical world, as you call it? I will explain to you why. The Light within every cell of your body, which is the Light Pattern, is the Limitless "Mighty I AM Presence." Therefore, Dear Hearts, that which you clothe those Great Points of Light with, is of human creation and is that which the world, the outer world, has been calling the physical world. Now do you not see how, in the acceptance of your "Mighty I AM Presence," you are accepting the Light Pattern of your physical body which has no imperfection in It?

As your attention is kept on the "Presence," the Light expands; and the human, the clothing or density with which you have clothed It, steadily and surely dissolves and disappears. It is a Law of Life! It is not a matter of someone's belief. It is a Law of Life — your Life and all Life! It is the same way with all Life in Nature. As individuals among mankind accept the "Mighty I AM Presence" and call It into action to produce Perfection in their lives and world, all Nature must also take on the Perfection which mankind has called forth. That is why you will find such great changes taking place in Nature. There will be greater beauty and greater distribution of moisture throughout the Earth, and balance all that kind of thing. It will be quite noticeable after the seventh of April.

Now, Dear Ones, mankind has always sought some Manifestation to prove the Existence, the Authority, if you please, of these Great Cosmic Beings, the Ascended Masters, the Great Legion of Light, and all those Great Beings who have ministered so long to the Earth. Well, there are constant Manifestations, but people do not accept Them. They do not accept the Reality of Them — but instead, use every excuse to keep from acknowledging this Mighty Law of Life, and when something occurs, say it just happened. Now for instance, when the Messengers were in Dallas, a Great Manifestation of Light occurred and dozens of people saw It; but the most of them said, "Well, I think that must have occurred from something outside." You see, humanity is held in its own ignorance because of the great doubts and fears which have accumulated in the mental and feeling world of mankind. Until humanity will take the determined stand to acknowledge this Light of the "Mighty I AM Presence," it will continue in the bondage of its own doubts and fears. You had better make a mistake a few times in accepting a thing as an Inner Activity and find it was of the outer activity, than once fail to acknowledge and receive an Inner Manifestation of the Real! I do not mean you must be gullible, not at all; but unless you get into the habit of accepting these Great Cosmic Manifestations and these Great Inner Powers, how in the world will you have the manifestation of Them?

Your attention is the powerhouse in accepting these things. Your Power of Qualification is acting all the time; and if you do not begin to accept these Greater Activities, how can you have Them manifest in your Life? The power of acceptance is a tremendous thing, as well as is your attention; but if you will give your attention earnestly to your "Presence," you will receive individually all the Manifestation you require—peacefully, gently, and in small ways. Then surely will come forth the great Manifestations which will clear forever all doubt from your being.

So, Dear Ones, I want you today to feel that you are no longer bound in any way. Do not fail *ever,* Dear Ones, before you retire at night—please, I plead with you—call on the Law of Forgiveness for any mistakes you have ever made; whether you know of them or not makes no difference. Then say: " 'Mighty I AM Presence,' charge my world with Your Wondrous Perfection. While this body sleeps, through my Higher Mental Body pour forth such Mighty Rays and Radiance of Light into my world, that every human creation and discordant thing there is dissolved forever!"

Precious Ones, you do not yet have but a fragmentary realization of what you could do. You are really God Beings and, once you really feel that, can experience your full Freedom.

Now We are going to take up more definitely how, during sleep, you can charge your Higher Mental Body to act—or charge your "Presence" to act through your Higher Mental Body—to cleanse, purify, and set things in order in your world, in your home, or wherever it is necessary. Do you not see, Precious Ones, that while your body sleeps there are no doubts, fears, or resistance acting within your human self?

When you charge your "Presence," through your Higher Mental Body, to act while your body sleeps, ofttimes you will awaken in the morning with a Perfect Glory blazing through you during the day and flowing out into your world.

You must see, Precious Ones, that the only obstruction that exists in your world today is in your waking state, through your feeling—accumulated feeling which We call human creation. Now then, do you not see, Dear Ones, step by step We find you ready to take hold of your Dominion with a firmer grasp, in the Acknowledgment of your "Presence"? Soon, Precious Ones, you must be wholly free from everything that binds you, even in the world of human activity. After all, as the dissolving of your human takes place, you act in a world no longer human, but Divine; and that Divine Activity will become your world of action in the years ahead of you. When the fullness of the Golden Age has come in, then you will no longer be acting through the human but only the Divine in you, which is your "Mighty I AM Presence."

Now notice: Why do I call your attention to this Higher Activity today? Because the Heart in your human body represents your "Mighty I AM Presence" in action right here—the same as America is the Heart of the World, the Earth. So your Heart is the Anchorage and Activity of your "Mighty I AM Presence," right here in your physical form. Now let us feel this very powerfully, and no longer accept that any other power can act but the Light right here from your "Mighty I AM Presence."

Students have so often asked, when contemplating old terminology, "Why is it so necessary not to mix this with other teaching?" This is why I said to you, Dear Hearts, who have studied occult and various forms of metaphysics, to put aside everything else you ever studied. Please do not intrude old terminology into this. Just take this in the simplicity and the clearness with which Saint Germain has brought It forth; and know that right here [pointing to the Heart] is my "Mighty I AM Presence" in action—right here. Then do you not see the feeling of health, perfecting of conditions, or anything you require is right here in your Heart, ready to act and produce that which you require? If you will think of It in that way, you will see how much more powerful It is. While it is true that the greater part of your "Mighty I AM Presence" is above you, yet this part of you is anchored right here in your Heart; and as you give attention to It, this part expands until in one sweep all can be dissolved which has been limiting or discordant.

Do not limit your ability to call your "Presence" into action with such intensity that all things are quickly dissolved which are less than Perfection. See! The reason I am saying this today is that so many times the Students write the Messengers and say: "Well, I know what you are going to tell me, but I do not quite feel I have the ability you have to call the 'Presence' into action." Well, that really is not the case. You do have the ability, only you just do not think so, you see? As long as you put it off for somebody else to call your "Presence" into action, just that much longer you are depriving yourself of the quick freedom you would have in your own determined Call to the "Presence."

Now notice, Precious Ones! Your determination is the Activity of the Inner Will of the "Mighty I AM Presence." Therefore in your Call you do not have to tear your hair out, you know; but call with firm determination, and accept in your feelings that your "Mighty I AM Presence" answers this right now. In a little while you will gain such Victory and confidence that every time you make a Call, within a few hours, a day or two, the Answer will be there. We have the proof of it constantly.

In the activity of the Messenger here, it has been so very marked. Oh, I assure you, he was more timid than most of you. When this Transformation has taken place in his Life, then there is not one of you that cannot have equally as great Accomplishment; but remember his willing, absolute willing Obedience has been the great and quick Victory for him.

Notice, Precious Ones—you know how mankind does overlook things. The Great Divine Director, Jesus, and Saint Germain have asked the Students to live according to the Group regulations. Yet again, again, and again, they come back and say, "Well, I wonder if I could not do this?" Notice the Obedience of this Good Messenger. He never questions. When They ask him to do a certain thing, he forgets everything else and does the thing They require. If the beloved Students would just do that joyously and willingly, they would see such manifestations; but as long as they want to intrude their own ideas, they are not obedient. They do not always know this—and it is not criticism, but We must explain it in the endeavor to correct the feeling which is acting within some individuals. Now, Saint Germain's Work explains Itself absolutely! Yet individuals feel that they can add to It and give a clearer explanation. It is a funny thing, is it not? They are perfectly sincere; but it is the habit of the human to feel that it understands a little better than the other fellow and can give a little clearer explanation. You see? Well, sometimes it does seem to be so; but after all, Dear Hearts, you cannot live the Life of the other individual. Make them do some work! You know the human always wants to lie down on the job and "let George do it"; but you will find, Precious Ones, you cannot do that. When you come to a certain point, you must buckle on your armor and get busy in your application. Then you will quickly be free.

My Joy is so great for this opportunity of speaking to you Heart to Heart; for these are, oh, so real —how real, Precious Ones, are these Heart-to-Heart talks. Only in time to come will you realize how truly they are Heart-to-Heart talks, because My Heart is acting within yours while you are here today. Oh, is it not a wonderful thing to feel the Heartthrob of your blessed Hearts—notice, the Hearts of the "Mighty I AM Presence"! That Heart in you is not yours! Did you ever think about that? It is the Heart of your "Mighty I AM Presence." Yet some of you think you have Heart trouble. Is it not comical what the human will do? Now in the future, I know every precious one of you will never again think of yourself, your outer self, that you do not think of your Heart as the Heart of the "Mighty I AM Presence." That is true, absolutely true! It is not your Heart. *I mean that!* You think it belongs to you; but it is that which gives you Life and therefore belongs to the "Presence."

Now then! Now then, watch out here! We are getting down now to definite things. You accept that this is the Heart of your "Mighty I AM Presence." Then let us go a little farther. Within are the points of Light in every cell of your body which have to come from the Heart. Then that also belongs to your "Mighty

I AM Presence," does it not? Now look out! Then, what is there left that does not belong to your "Presence"? Just this covering with which you have clothed those Points of Light—the cells of your body.

You do not quite yet realize it, but those cells of your body would respond to you instantly if you would only realize it. They would absolutely obey you as quick as a flash if you only had the confidence that they would do it. It is because you have so long forgotten you are Master of your body, that the cells say, "Oh, I have got something to say about this!" But they really have not—they are just putting it over on you, they are running a bluff on you. You notice, I am getting very like you in My Expressions, but I want you to feel how close We are to you. Do you think it any disgrace if We use your expressions? If you do, why can We not? I want you to *feel* We are not far off, for We are going to make you *feel* that We are the Reality before We get through. I rejoice today to see in your Hearts the wonderful acceptance of Our Reality, more and still more than has ever been there before; and you know what that means? It means more and more quickly you go forth into Absolute Freedom from all limitations of every kind.

Oh, just feel now as I draw, or cause the Messenger to draw, his hand over his body, will you just *feel* this now? Let Me give you this Assistance, will you not?

" 'Mighty I AM Presence,' sweep out of everyone every limiting discordant thing! Consume it in the Violet Consuming Flame this instant! And set each one free in the clear comprehension and feeling of his own 'Mighty I AM Presence' as the only Activity within his human form or world." Again: " 'Mighty I AM Presence!' Sweep out of these human forms every limiting, discordant thing! Quickly dissolve and consume all discord in the Violet Consuming Flame!"

" 'Mighty I AM Presence,' sweep through each human form! Sweep out every imperfection and every limitation that is within each one's consciousness! Replace this by the Ascended Masters' Substance and Intelligence to act there with full Power henceforth, to produce quickly the Mighty Manifestations of the 'Mighty I AM Presence' when called into Action. Hold Thy Dominion in the feeling world and give everyone this Mighty Confidence in their 'Mighty I AM Presence,' Its full Power and Ability to do everything they ask It to do which is constructive!" No Student of the "I AM" would ask his "Presence" to do anything that was not constructive; and if they do, the "Presence" would not do it. Therefore, when We call the "Presence" into Action, We take it for granted that all want only constructive activity. Therefore, We bring into action today this Activity of the "Mighty I AM Presence" released within the Heart of the individual, to expand throughout the body quickly, expand throughout the home and world of activity, and to take command and hold Its Dominion there. Will you, every one, accept that and feel It henceforth all-powerfully active?

I extend to you the Greetings of the Great Host of Ascended Masters, the Mighty Legion of Light, the Great Angelic Host, the Great Angel Devas, Gods of the Mountains, the God of Gold, and the God of Light! In every age wherein great Perfection has reigned, gold has been in generous use because it is Pure, Life-giving Energy. Again mankind will come to use it freely in beautifying and decorating their buildings and homes.

Today let us accept forever all that is required, whether it be money, confidence, courage, happiness —whatever it may be! Let us accept the fullness of the "Mighty I AM Presence" flooding our world with it. It is for the use of all, Beloved Ones. You cannot be limited in the Acknowledgment of your "Presence"; whether it be money you require, courage, confidence, Life, health, or strength—it is there. Think of it! Does that sound like a paradox?

In your Heart is all the gold you require for use. Do you realize, Precious Ones, there are three ac-tivities of gold? The metallic gold that you find in the Earth, the liquified gold that has often been used in a very wondrous manner in those former days of Per-fection, and then the Essence of Gold which is your

Life. I venture, earnest as you are, perhaps not a single one of you has realized when We ask you to flood yourself with the Golden Light, that It is the Essence from which metallic gold comes. Think of it! Think of it! You are using gold in its three activities; and then mankind will take each others' lives for a few dollars of gold—when they are filled with it all the time! Perhaps these individuals have not quite so much of it, but still they have some.

I rejoice, Precious Ones, that you go forth different beings today, glorified with so much greater courage and confidence in your Application, in your ability, in your feeling that every limitation is absolutely gone down before you, and your pathway is one of Wondrous Light in which there is no human obstruction. Will you not feel that and picture it before you? If there is any shadow attempts to come into that Light, say: "Oh, no you don't; you are finished! I walk in this Pathway of my 'Mighty I AM Presence,' and there is no human creation of mine or anybody else's that is going to enter into that again." Use your determination again! Will you not do that for Me? For yourself?

My Joy is boundless for this humble Service which it has been My privilege to render today. Carry It with you always into your Full Victory. Then one day when We meet in that Great Octave of Light—you, free Ascended Beings—then I shall shake your hand

and welcome you there! Until then, We shall often hold your hand in the closing pilgrimage upon Earth for you, and give you, through Our Radiation, that Freedom, Courage, and Confidence of your Victory; for God, the "Mighty I AM Presence" in you, is your Certain Victory always. I thank you.

MRS. RAYBORN'S DISCOURSE

WOODARDS' GROUP — LOS ANGELES, CALIFORNIA

MARCH 21, 1937

— AFTERNOON —

BELOVED Students of the Light, you who have read *Unveiled Mysteries, The Magic Presence* — those Books of the experience of this Good Messenger — will need no introduction to Myself. You know that at the time of My Ascension, not a single thing of this kind in the Western World had yet been made public. Even My own beloved family thought I was still in the tomb, after the Beloved Saint Germain had released Me from it. It was a very wonderful thing.

Today will you bear with Me, because this is the day of the Ascension Work for these Beloved Ones who are conducting this Class. I want to bring this to your notice and show you how this beloved one had arranged today really for My coming. She might not have known it, yet it was done — just the same as Mr. Frank Lanning unknowingly prepared the way for the Mighty Arcturus.

Now Dear Ones, the Ascension is so practical. When My body lay first in the home and then in the receptacle which had been prepared for it, I was free

136

from that body, discussing with Saint Germain the plans for My Ascension. Please feel, as I speak these Words to you, the Reality of My own Experience; for It will carry into your feeling world the conviction of how practical and how real the Ascension is. That must one day be achieved by every human being on Earth. It is not a matter of your choice, Beloved Ones; but the Eternal Victory over the conditions of the Earth comes finally through the Ascension.

Now there are many, many among the "I AM" Students in America today who can make that same Ascension which I did, in this embodiment. Why do you suppose this Good Messenger was brought to the Cave of Symbols, permitted to witness these Transcendent Activities and to assist in one? So he might carry back to mankind the feeling of that True Reality. Jesus, the Beloved One, conveyed It to mankind two thousand years ago or more; but who believed It? Now in our Western World, our Beloved America, there has come the same proof to mankind. Today there will be further proof, because the time is not far distant when a number of the Ascended Masters will come and make Their Bodies, Their Ascended Bodies, tangible to you so that all may see and know the Truth of which the Messengers have spoken.

Now then, in My Endeavor to convey into your feeling world the Reality which I know to be, will you through your feeling accept this—the Radiation which My Words, as Cups, carry to you? Accept It! and allow It to do Its Perfect Work within your mind and body.

Believe Me, Beloved Ones, when I say that the sense of years over your head really makes no difference. You do not know what your "Mighty I AM Presence" can do for you. Please do not limit It. I know how I had limited Myself, believing I was entering so-called death. Yet there is no such thing in the Universe as death, oh, Beloved Ones! I say this to you precious ones with the silver hair: There is no death, never was, and never can be. It is true individuals cast off their bodies, but you are more alive then than you are in the limited body.

Now this Great Blessing which has come to mankind through the Beloved Saint Germain is giving humanity the full conscious conviction of their own ability to enter into the Ascended Masters' State of Eternal Freedom. Let Me say for your great strength and encouragement that in the interim when I lost consciousness for a few moments in the outer, and then became vividly conscious in My Higher Mental Body, it was a state of consciousness never to be forgotten. I thought it was a long time. Yet I was only a few moments entering from the state of outer consciousness into the full Consciousness of My Higher Mental Body—notice this—in which I was able to give Saint Germain the assistance He required in enabling Me to make My Ascension. Saint Germain could not make that Ascension for Me; but He, in the unlimited Activity of My Higher Mental Body, taught Me how to release the Currents of Energy quickly from My "Presence," which did the work of refining the part of My physical body which it was necessary to raise into My Higher Mental Body.

Thus We become the Ascended Being. Remember it is the refined part of your physical bodies that Ascends and is absorbed into your Higher Mental Body. At this point, the Transformation from the human into the Divine takes place! All appearance of age leaves your body and the garments you are wearing dissolve into the Garments of the Higher Octave. Then as the Great Ray of Light and Energy descends from the "Mighty I AM Presence," the refined part of your physical body — and mark you, there is nothing left behind — the refined part of your physical body Ascends. It is absorbed into your Higher Mental Body. It Ascends on this Ray of Light from your "Presence" and is absorbed into the Electronic Body of your "Mighty I AM Presence." Then you become the Ascended Being, such as I am today, as Jesus, Saint Germain, and hundreds of other Ascended Beings are.

There is only one Process, Beloved Ones, by which this is accomplished. I have given you the exact

Explanation, as the Messenger has and always does in the Classes. Feel how practical this is and that It is within your reach. Oh, do not let the matter of years interfere with your feeling of the full consciousness of your ability to have this Victory. Do you see now the Beauty of that which Saint Germain has brought forth? We have all used this same Application to accomplish the end of this human pilgrimage, which is the Ascension. Please feel that your human no longer has power to limit you, even in your comprehension of these simple yet majestic Truths. Feel now that the Ascension is for you!

Returning again to My own Experience: It was made clear to Me how, by directing certain Currents of Energy from My "Presence," I could—instead of releasing Myself from the body—by those Mighty Currents purify that body which lay there apparently helpless, and then raise it into its Eternal Perfection and Activity.

Precious Ones, the day you experience that, it will never be forgotten in Eternity. Oh, the thrill of the Victory when you begin to see the change through the Rays! In My case, I was in My Higher Mental Body pouring these Rays forth on the body which I thought, as the outer memory closed and the Inner began, I was leaving behind. As I turned and from the Higher Mental Body began to project those Rays, I watched in every cell of that body the change which took place. I watched the Light renewing it and installing or expanding the Life, the Light within each cell; and I watched the density with which I had clothed it dissolve. Then to see that body raise and come to Me! Thank you for feeling that so vividly. I feel greatly rejoiced that you can feel the Reality which I wish to convey to you. It will always remain, Beloved Ones, within your feeling world, and I greatly appreciate it.

My humble Efforts today will not have been in vain, for I rejoice that so many of you can accept It fully! Allow It to become active in your Life to do Its Perfect Work in your body.

The Great Ascended Masters assisting and the Beloved Saint Germain, who has such Courage, brought forth this Work and stood guard over It until now. It is expanding the Light in these Groups, which this Beloved Messenger has found he could come to and voice Our Wishes to you. Far more than that, It carries into your feeling world the Reality which We know to be for your Blessing.

So in this Activity today there is another great step of Achievement. Do you wonder, you who are so greatly in earnest, why certain Ones of the Ascended Masters are using this opportunity to dictate and convey Their Wishes to you? Because a very definite, powerful Accomplishment is being set into action within you for your Victory. When this Class at the

Pan Pacific Auditorium is completed, there will be hundreds of you precious ones who will not again know limitations. Oh, I rejoice so greatly!

At the time I returned and sang in the Ascended Body, as described in *The Magic Presence*, you could never know the Joy, the "thrill" as you express it, which filled My Being in again being able to stand forth visible and tangible in the limitless Power of the Voice of My "Mighty I AM Presence." Today there are hundreds of the blessed, beloved "I AM" Students who are beginning to sing with that Inner Voice. Oh, that suddenly all human sense of limitation might be removed, so you could *feel* the full Glory of your "Mighty I AM Presence" as It stands ready to pour forth through your Heart Its Wondrous Glory! Your Heart is the Heart of the "Mighty I AM Presence" — Its Anchorage within your human form.

May I say to you, as the Great Arcturus said today, "Your Heart is not *your* Heart, but the Heart of the 'Mighty I AM Presence.' " How well I found that out when I saw that through my human Heart in the form which lay there seemingly helpless, I could restore, purify it quickly, and raise it into Eternal Freedom. I am using that same purified Ascended Body today and always shall. You do not, after you have made the Ascension in this manner, ever return into human embodiment again. It is not necessary!

Your pilgrimage on Earth is finished, but you can come and make that body tangible and visible at will in the octave of Earth. You can render a Service indescribable and inconceivable to the one not yet having attained.

Today My Joy is very great in being able to convey into your feeling world the Reality of this which I am describing to you of My own Experience. Why do I speak of Myself? Because I can thus convey to you the True Feeling I had at the time of the Accomplishment.

Now you will go forward in the deeper and deeper Understanding of your "Mighty I AM Presence." You will be more conscious of your ability to call It forth much more powerfully each day. Know that your Application cannot fail when you call your "Mighty I AM Presence" into Action. The Power of the Universe surges into action to fulfill your requirement! It knows no interference or resistance. Then you realize your part is to keep your feeling world harmonious until the "Presence" can do the thing for which you have called. In that, you know positively It cannot fail. As you gain this confidence, you will go from one wondrous Victory to another, and with very great speed.

When I saw the distress within My loved ones who had been left behind, I said to Saint Germain, "Is there not some way We can alleviate that?" He said,

"Oh, yes." Then, We went into the home where My blessed family were together. He showed Me how to release peace and rest through the Power of Radiation to the family, and quickly they became adjusted.

Then shortly after, when Saint Germain one day said to Me (I had not yet discovered this Myself), "Great Joy is in store for you," I asked, "Just what do you mean?" And He replied, "There is going to be another Ascension in your family," and I exclaimed, "Can you mean it?" Then He showed Me how it was to be accomplished, and My Rejoicing knew no bounds. During that Accomplishment, I went with Saint Germain to the Cave of Symbols. There in the tangible, visible Body, I held My own two beloved children in My Fond Embrace. Again, can you not imagine, can you not feel even now as I speak, Our great Rejoicing?

Oh, there is no experience of grief, Dear Hearts. That is only what the human has conceived and made real to the outer consciousness. Today, this great Infinite Knowledge and Understanding is being made real, simple, and plain to beloved humanity. Our Love is so great for you. Having gone the way and knowing how wonderful is the Achievement, do you think We could ever rest until you too were all Ascended into the same Great Freedom? Oh, no! No one who has accomplished the Great Victory feels satisfied until all of those blessed ones following on have also achieved this same Great Victory.

The Mighty Divine Director and the other Blessed Ones who have come forth have charged into the feeling world of mankind these Great Qualities. They always see within your world the Assistance which They can give, of which you are not yet aware. How you will thank the Messengers one day, when with that clear Inner Vision you see what their great courageous effort has been to bring Saint Germain's Freedom and Blessing to mankind. There is no Rejoicing in the whole Universe so great.

So, step by step, Beloved Ones, with all the Power the Law of your being permits, We are conveying steadily and surely into your feeling world that which will be your certain, complete and — We hope — quick Victory. It will be rapid to the degree that you will, through your feeling world, say to all limiting discordant appearances, "You have no power!" and really feel that is true. Then as you call your "Mighty Presence" into action to perform any given Service, you will find that the Intelligent Energy of your "Presence" will act with tremendously greater Power and Speed, because there is no feeling within you to obstruct the way. Your discordant feeling is the only thing in the whole Universe, so far as your world is concerned, that can obstruct your way. You see, within you is the Victory or the failure.

Here is the great encouragement in the Understanding, Activity, and acceptance of your "Mighty I AM Presence" today. Let us take for an example one who only partially feels the Reality of his own "Mighty I AM Presence." One day he thinks, "I believe that is true"—and tomorrow, "I am not so sure about it." That person is wavering and will not have the quick Victory. Suppose he says, "I know that 'Presence' is there, and nothing shall take that away from me." Then he enters into a positive state, and he will receive the Power more quickly. With the one who has been wavering, once he has contemplated the Chart, the Heart knows Its Reality. If he does not gain the Victory in this embodiment, then he certainly will in the next.

This is the beauty, the wonder of this Understanding of your "Presence." Whatever you do not gain in this embodiment when you go forth free from the body, you will carry with you clearly and vividly—all you have gained in the Understanding of your "Mighty I AM Presence." Then when you have cast off the body, you stand free. Thus, the Ascended Masters will take you into Their Octave of Light. They will complete the full feeling within you of your Reality and the Victory. When you come back into your next embodiment, you will quickly gain your Victory and the Ascension. That is why, Precious Ones, this Understanding is so powerful and far-reaching. Every step you gain in the Acknowledgment of your "Presence" is Eternal. You never lose it! Nor can you ever forget it — I mean within your feeling world.

You know, the intellect is a very curious actor. It jumps from place to place out here and only judges from the appearances; but the Heart stands steady and firm. *It knows!* It never jumps from one thing to the other. It is always accepting the "Mighty I AM Presence"; but the intellect, through its ability to judge from partial information, makes constant mistakes. It says to the Heart, "Oh no, no! These things cannot be true." But the Heart goes serenely on, ignoring its attitude, knowing some day, somewhere, that intellect will have to subside and give obedience to the "Presence." That allows the Power of the Heart to act in Its Fullness. Then comes the Freedom! Then comes the Joy which fills the Hearts of all mankind.

Our precious Lady Betty is having a day of real work, but how she is being blessed in that work. I want her, Lady Betty, to know how joyously We have stood guard to give her Assistance to her Complete Victory. She is winning It in a wonderful manner. Her wonderful, limitless service in the Staff has been so beautiful. You precious ones in your way too are winning that Great Victory.

Our Blessed "Little Dynamite," as some of the Students have come to call the Blessed Messenger Mrs. Ballard — how We love her! You cannot imagine,

Precious Ones, that dauntless, limitless, courageous Service which she is rendering—working all day and all night in getting the things ready that give you Blessing and Freedom. Even today, when she would so love to be present, she is working on the Decree Book to have those Decrees ready for you, to help you all possible to your Freedom.

Oh, We want you to know, Blessed Ones, how We love you; how the Messengers and the Staff love you; how grateful is Our Love to you for your love which you pour out to the Messengers and Ourselves. You have heard the Statement so often: " 'I AM' the Open Door which no man can shut." Do you know what that really means? Your outpouring of love is the Open Door, because that Love comes from your "Mighty I AM Presence." Your outpouring of love is the Open Door which no man can shut; for it keeps you a pure, open channel for the Glorious Radiance and Energy from your "Presence" to pour forth to bless you.

In closing, let Me say to you: do not accept, Precious Ones, ever again the lack of energy in your bodies. Do not do that! It is only your human concept which limits you. Oh, just like that [wave of hand], burst every human thing that is binding you! Allow the Great Energy from the "Presence" to flow through—and It will at your Call. Try it! Say: " 'Mighty I AM Presence!' Charge my mind and body with Your Limitless Energy, with Your Perfect Health! You are the Perfect Action of my body, 'Mighty I AM Presence'—I had forgotten that; but now, since I know it, I will not accept anything else into my world but Your Perfect Activity." If one has a sense of age, it will quickly disappear. You would feel the joyous activity of a young girl. It is possible for you to do that and quickly! The gentlemen may do the same!

Do you remember the old Statement Our Blessed One made: "Except ye become as little children, ye cannot enter the Kingdom"? Do you not see, Precious Ones, what is meant by that? As you become consciously aware of your "Presence" and are able to release Its Energy at your Call—the Limitless Energy from your "Presence"—do you not see that you have youth and freedom of action? Although you are grown in form, you are as little children in the activity of your freedom and the alertness of your intellect. This is a very wonderful thing. It is here for the use of all who really accept it.

Saint Germain, the Great Master from Venus, Nada, the Divine Director, and I have recently discussed this very Activity. We are trusting that the Great Cosmic Law will permit certain things to be done for certain of the "I AM" Students, to be an example for the rest. That which I referred to above is one of them. We may take one who shows the appearance

of perhaps sixty years—you know that is quite young
these days. Then We would quickly bring about the
Transformation of Eternal Youth in appearance as
well as activity, that mankind may see the result of
the Power of their "Presence" and what It can do for
them. A few examples of that kind, I am sure, would
be absolute and complete liberation of mankind.
There will no doubt be many things done which will
give the evidence.

You know the human. Oh, it wants evidence so
much, and yet within its own human form is the greatest evidence of the Universe. The very anchorage of
Life in the human form is the greatest proof possible.
There could be no greater evidence, if individuals but
knew it; but still there are being planned many things
for humanity which will more quickly enable them
to accept the great Outpouring from the "Presence"
and give them the quick Victory.

I rejoice in this opportunity, in My humble way,
to give Assistance to you today. I thank the beloved
sister Mrs. Woodard for the opportunity of expressing My Wishes; to you, Precious Ones, for being able
to accept it, for I am so rejoiced at the great acceptance you have been able to feel of My humble Efforts.
Will you not carry this with you constantly—My Feeling, My Presence of your Victory?

Think of it! Only very recently, Dear Hearts, was
My Victory accomplished—only just a few years ago.

Think of it! It is not from some far-off age that I come to tell you of My Victory. The Beloved Saint Germain invited Me to come, because in so recent an Achievement He says He thinks I can convey more quickly and clearly into your feeling world that which is your Victory, because it was Mine also. Today, I rejoice with all My Heart, and I shall have to stop or our Beloved Lady Betty will run out of books.

We just love you with a Love that is a Mighty Dissolving Activity, dissolving every imperfection which has existed in your world. Will you not accept It? In the use of the Violet Consuming Flame, call your "Presence" into action to complete the Activity quickly. Then stand forth joyous and free; for God, the "Mighty I AM Presence" in you—in your Heart—is your certain Victory! I thank you.

TALL MASTER FROM VENUS'
DISCOURSE

ROGERS' GROUP — LOS ANGELES, CALIFORNIA

MARCH 21, 1937

— EVENING —

BELOVED Ones of Earth, how rejoiced We are on Our far distant Planet at the Expansion of your Light on Earth. Do you think it so strange that One might be in your presence from that far distant Planet, Venus? Yet if you consider it for just a moment, to Us who are free of limitations, distance, as you know it, is not considered. I know it is not easy for you to comprehend that just yet, but you will. One day you will understand as clearly as We do how, as you enter into your Freedom which is your "Mighty I AM Presence," you transcend time and space. Then the so-called far distant Planets are so near.

You must realize, Precious Ones, that the Ascended Master, as you have been told many times, does not recognize time—or space. Even this Good Messenger, as he went from place to place with Saint Germain, did not; for they went from one part of the Earth to another in from two to three minutes, in that body which Saint Germain created for his use.

Will you try earnestly not to analyze? Just feel for you there is no longer time nor space. If you can do that, you will enter into your complete Freedom so much more quickly.

Shall I tell you just how I feel tonight? It is as if We were in a great schoolroom and you were having your graduation exercises. That really is true. You are, Beloved Ones of Earth, entering into your Freedom! As I speak these Words tonight, will you be kind enough to accept My Radiance which I pour forth into your feeling world to enable you to feel fully the assurance of that? You are entering now into your full Freedom. I say to you, that no longer can human creations bind you in any way.

Oh, the joy which floods the room as I speak those Words! It shall act with definite Power until you fully realize, feel satisfied, and find manifest in your outer world of activity all the Perfection which is there. We must know that! You beloved ones have been willing and have joyfully entered in to the requirements for this Great Perfection, making a condition for Our Reception which you do not yet comprehend. You will one day know what that means.

We find the Earth ready, willing, and humbly accepting the Great Assistance which the Wondrous Kumaras have so long poured forth in Their Mighty Radiance to the Earth. We, Myself included, are but children in comparison to the Great Kumaras who came forth so many hundreds of thousands of years ago to assist the Earth and to hold it in balance, until enough of its Children could be raised into Perfection and hold the balance themselves within the Earth. This is being rapidly accomplished now, and ere long Their Work will be finished. When it is, there will be thousands in America who will see Sanat Kumara stand before them in the tangible, visible Body—a Youth as of sixteen summers.

As you were told today, regardless of your silver hair, regardless of your appearance of age that sometimes seems to weigh heavily upon you, if you but realized it, you could shatter all appearances and human accumulation. In a few hours you could stand in Eternal Youth, Beauty, and Perfection. Mankind has forgotten its dominion because individuals have forgotten the Light, the Life, the Intelligence, the Energy which gives them Life, Eternal Youth, and Beauty. Is it not a pity that mankind has forgotten this? Life knows no age! Energy knows no age! Substance knows no age! Then what is it which feels age? Just the limited human concepts, because mankind has forgotten that everyone is really a Divine Being.

Tonight as I speak to you, please feel the Radiance from each Word entering into your being to become all-powerfully Active there, that you may hold the Substance of that which I convey to you all-powerfully Active within you. Oh, Dear Ones, you must realize that it is not just the Words which We flash before the Messenger which are important. They are but to hold your attention while the great Inner Work is being done. All words are cups carrying certain qualities, but the far greater activity is in the Inner Radiation which goes forth into your world. Is it necessary for Me to remind you tonight that in your Acknowledgment of your "Mighty I AM Presence," all Its Great Activity takes place from within out? Therefore the great accomplishment, and greater percent of it, is accomplished within, before you become aware of it without. Your activity has previously just reversed that. You have tried to act from without in, and of course entered into greater and greater limitations; but when you realize that your Heart is the Presence of the "Mighty I AM" acting within you, then you must know that It would produce Perfection for you if there were not something acting within your feeling world which was clothing It with less than Its full Perfection. Hold close to this now, so you can have forever dismissed from your feeling world everything —so not one thing longer limits you.

We are making a tremendous Effort to free a certain number of mankind for that which is to follow! You beloved ones here, of your own volition have entered into a joyous willingness to make yourselves ready for this. Then you invite Us to come and give every Assistance possible.

To this Beloved Brother We give great, great credit for having been the means of establishing an Activity with such great volume, through which We can do certain things that will not only give yourselves freedom, but will spread the Light forth powerfully to give others freedom. When I say "freedom," I do not mean just one thing, but Complete Freedom from every limiting thing that has ever been in your feeling world or its activity.

You beloved ones who have entered these wondrous closed Groups have entered into a new world. It is also quite wonderful to see those who are really wonderful, sincerely honest with themselves, yet who feel that they are not quite ready to enter this Great Activity. So We bless all and keep on pouring forth Our Encouragement to strengthen them, until they too will feel themselves quite strong enough and ready to enter into the fuller and greater Activity which is their freedom.

I try to find Words to convey My Feeling to you of the Joy I have in coming into your midst and seeing such a great Light within you, for only a few short years ago the atmosphere about you was comparatively dense. In 1900 when We came (unknown to the people of Earth) and looked over humanity, We saw so few whose Light had expanded until It could be amplified to give them strength, courage, and dominion. We found it could not be done then

(I am taking you especially into My Confidence tonight), and We had to withdraw. Then Sanat Kumara said to Us: "The time will come, possibly nearer than you think at present, when You can give the Assistance which is needed." Sure enough, in His Great Wisdom that day has arrived!

Oh, Beloved Children of Earth, you can scarcely comprehend before your Ascension, what you owe to Our Beloved Saint Germain. He has, because of His great Courage, brought this Light and Freedom to you and mankind. Will you remember the description of Him which the Messengers have read to you from the *Fire of Creation*? Read it often, Dear Hearts, and see what a Mighty Being He is from your Earth. Remember, Saint Germain is a product of your Earth; and in spite of all of Us, He had the Conviction, the Courage, the Strength to stand before a great Group of Us and say, "I shall try out that which I feel!" — and His Victory came!

I say this to you tonight, Beloved Ones, because of the many people from the orthodox world who cannot quite understand why Saint Germain should take a place with Jesus. Dear Ones, Jesus is doing His Mighty Work, and so is Saint Germain. As the beloved Charles Sindelar has placed Them hand in hand in the magazine, so do They act for the Children of Earth. Remember that, Dear Hearts! In spite of anyone, Saint Germain must have credit for the Courage which led Him to try out that which has become a success for mankind in setting individuals free.

Unless you do this, you will but delay your Freedom. Not that He is even interested whether you give Him credit or not; but the Law of your Life and your Earth is that credit must be given where it is due, and an acknowledgment must come forth from mankind for what has been accomplished. That Law of Life for your Earth is irrevocable! It is imperative, because mankind has drawn away from Perfection. Of their own Free Will, all individuals must come back through gratitude and acknowledgment, giving credit to Those who lift them out of the limitations into which they have drawn themselves.

Once you understand clearly these Mighty Fundamentals, then you will enter much more quickly and easily into your Freedom. Think of it, Beloved Children of Earth! In the Assistance which is given you today, the effort of attainment is a thousand percent less than it was at the time Saint Germain and those of Us who are assisting attained Our Freedom and Ascension. Now mark you, that is comparatively recent. Does a few hundred years seem a long time to you? Well, a few thousand years does not seem long to Us. Why does it seem long?

Now, let us come down to your human experiences before you entered into this Understanding of the "Mighty I AM Presence." For a moment remind yourself of how many times, time — notice — *time* hung heavy upon your hands. You did not know just what to do with yourself. Remember that! Then what happened? You began to conceive ideas to kill time. As the Great One Arcturus mentioned this today, may I repeat it to you again tonight? Do not ever use that word or expression again, "I want to kill time." You want to *transcend* time! Will you be kind enough to use that expression, "I want to transcend time"? Do you know that tonight you are really transcending time and space? Why? Because your attention is upon Me. I do not consider time nor space. It no longer exists for Me, and that is why I am here tonight — to help you to more quickly transcend time and space.

Now, what takes place in this Activity? First, you will find yourself doing the outer activities with a greater ease and a speed you had not before thought possible. Then you will find this, that, and the other thing is accomplished quickly. You will find much more time to give to your "Mighty I AM Presence"; and when you do have extra time, please do not spend it in playing bridge and such things. Oh, it is not that We do not want you to be happy — but see what your attention is upon! Do you know what is in your Earth's atmosphere concerning cards, and what your playing cards represent? The element of gambling. That is the general consciousness which pervades mankind, Dear Ones. Do you want to be a part of that consciousness? There are many other things through which you can have great Happiness. Now do not think that I am trying to take anything away from you of which you are fond. I am just citing to you the Law. We do not urge anyone to follow what We say, but We must cite the Law which is acting within you and your world.

In Our Activity upon Venus, We have the most wonderful rhythm in the dance, and music most exquisite; but never in any of those activities is there a thought of anything but Perfection—for as one enters into that great swing or rhythm of ecstasy and enjoyment, so does one learn to feel the Glories of the Rhythm of the Universe. Ere long, all broken rhythm will disappear from your Earth, for it has brought such distress upon mankind in recent years. It has shattered many hundreds of thousands! It has shattered the emotional bodies until they were unable to gather and hold sufficient cohesive activity to maintain their health. Thus has it shattered the forms, and they are lost so far as use to the individual is concerned.

Do you know why the majority of the savages in the jungle live so short a time? Because of the tom-tom rhythm that is in their jungle activities. Few live past middle age. Now and then one who through the feeling has conceived a certain part of the Law, lives to be sometimes eighty years old or a little more.

Try to comprehend the difference between that and the former activity. Before the Understanding of the Ascension was brought into the outer world, many, many of mankind maintained Life in the body for two, three, four, five, or six hundred years. The Beloved Cha Ara, who spoke at one of your Groups recently, maintained Life in His Body for five hundred years before He made the Ascension, because He had been One who came into that understanding through the old activity of the occult law, before it was My Privilege to set it aside for the Earth.

You know of the Messenger's unyielding stand on this point and have heard him speak so firmly of that night in the Royal Teton when I issued this Decree for the Earth which has gone forth. That Decree is doing a most wonderful Work for the Earth, and I shall forever bless this Good Messenger for the strength and courage with which he asserted the Cosmic Authority with which I give this forth to so many of mankind. Oh, how greatly We love and give praise and thanks for his courage and strength to go forth and carry this Message which means everything to mankind.

That old occult law had to fade from the Earth because of the wreckage it has wrought in mankind. I tell you, Dear Hearts, it has brought forth greater wreckage into humanity than you will ever know, because human concepts had crept in from every angle and, ofttimes, it was used to hold fear over mankind instead of to give freedom. Of course some of the occult teachers and students who had done that very thing were fierce in their attitude against this Good Brother, but they could not touch him.

So, Dear Ones, have all the courage in the world in calling your "Mighty I AM Presence" into action. Stand with firm determination by that which you call into action, for there is no means possible by which you can fail—in anything—when you call your "Mighty I AM Presence" into action.

I want to charge into your feeling world My very powerful Conviction that you cannot fail in a single instance, Dear Hearts, in your Application of your "Mighty I AM Presence." You cannot do it! I will not accept failure for any one of mankind! Every one of humanity shall apply this Law of the "Mighty I AM Presence" to their Eternal Freedom. I shall stand by It, for it was decreed that I be that Authority for the Earth; and having sent It forth, I stand back of It and of all of you until you have your Freedom.

There is naught in human creation that shall ever stop your freedom or that shall ever stop the Freedom of America. AMERICA SHALL BE FREE, FOREVER! There is naught in humanity that shall interfere with it. *Remember* all that seems to have such a desire is but an appearance; and you have been taught to say to all such appearances, "You have no power!" — and they have not!

Oh, Beloved Children of Earth, if once you understand the Authority that you have in all appearances of imperfection or destructive activity, and you say the moment they appear, "You have no power!" — then they have not, for you or your America. Do you not see, Beloved Children of Earth, when you issue that Mighty Decree, the Power of the Universe rushes forward into action to fulfill your requirement because you are calling for the Freedom of America through the Power of the "Mighty I AM Presence," which is a thousand times more powerful than anything that would bring destruction!

See how you have the full Power and Authority in issuing these Decrees, by saying to every appearance — whether it is individual, city, or nation — to every appearance that is less than Divine Justice, "You have no power!" Mean it! Feel it! And let that Mighty Decree go forth doing Its Perfect Work. You are yet, Beloved Ones, only partially aware of the Powerful Good which is in your hands in the acceptance of your "Presence," and in the issuing of these Decrees.

"Decree a thing and it shall be so unto you." Again feel these words: "Your outer determination is the Activity of your Inner Will, the 'Mighty I AM Presence.' " All of you have determination. If you become angry, have you not plenty of determination?

You are dauntless for that moment. Then, that same determination released on the constructive side of your activities becomes many times more powerful, because it is in agreement with the Law of Life. You can generate it and call it forth at will. Do not let your human intellect ever say to you, you cannot do it. *You can,* and you do realize it more each day. Use your determination to hold in obedience everything from your own human intellect, your human creations, or anyone else's, which would attempt to interfere with your Decree. Then you have become the Master of whatever you call forth into manifestation and action.

As you advance, oh, Beloved Ones, in a clearer, more definite understanding of the Power which is within your hands to use, through the Acknowledgment of your "Presence," you cannot make any mistake. There are a few who have tried to interfere with this Law and make false accusations against this Good Brother. They have been foolish enough to think they could, through their "Mighty I AM Presence," bring destruction to him. What nonsense! God help those unfortunate creatures who utter falsehood against his character! We stand back of him! And every human being on the face of this Earth that utters aught against him or his co-worker, shall swallow those words. Mark what I tell you!

Do you think when We have found those who

have been courageous enough to carry forth this Message, and then someone comes along and tries to besmirch their characters, that We shall stand idly by and see it attempted further? I want you to spread this Word to anybody who attempts to fill your mind with such falsehood.

He has been clean and pure enough to be able to receive Dictations from Beings who for thousands of years have been wholly Pure and Perfect. That any creature is so foolish as to attempt to spread falsehood concerning such a one's character is inconceivable. The foolishness of individuals who have once thought that they could bluff mankind into obedience to their nefarious work, proves they have lost their way. No longer does the bluff of human creation affect the Student of the Light! The pitiful thing is that those individuals shall reap the agony of that which they send forth, and nothing can prevent it because they have set it into action themselves.

I want you to know, oh, Beloved Ones, that the Light protects Its own! You are Children of the Light—"the Light of God that never fails!" Through your Call, and the use of the Violet Consuming Flame to keep all creation which has been drawn about you consumed before it finds expression, you will never find anything in the world that can harm you.

Remember, Precious Ones, that anything—accident or otherwise—which happens to an individual who has come into the Understanding of the "I AM Presence," can only come because there has not been sufficient use of the Violet Consuming Flame to keep the discordant creation—the past creation—dissolved as fast as it comes to the surface. That is the only reason. Now as mankind is coming more and more to understand the imperative need of calling the "Presence" into Action to use the Violet Consuming Flame for them, Students and individuals will always find themselves on guard and protected.

I thank you, Beloved Ones, and in the Great Love of My Being, I pour forth to you your Freedom, your Invincible Protection, your quick journey into Freedom from all limitations—and your Ascension. Will you not accept that from Me? To all, I say, do all your understanding permits to cooperate and have It as quickly as possible. I thank you.

MR. RAYBORN'S DISCOURSE

ANDREW'S 100% GROUP — GLENDALE, CALIFORNIA
MARCH 22, 1937

MOST Beloved Students of the Light and of the "Mighty I AM Presence," I consider it a very great privilege and joy to voice tonight that which has meant so much to Me. Not just in the accomplishment of the Ascension and My Freedom through It, but as I look upon the years that passed before, I see how much I was actually living in accordance with the Law, which I did not outwardly understand then.

I feel tonight that I should be able to convey to you how you too may have this same great Freedom of the Ascension, through those very experiences which were Mine. I know now that I intuitively knew, wholly through the Inner Prompting of the "Presence" that gave Me Life, the need of outer success in Life. I knew the need was to be humble, to be kind, yet firm in that which I knew to be right.

After the Ascension I was able to see how that Great Law of My "Mighty I AM Presence" was acting through Me unknowingly, by kindness. A natural quality within My human form kept Me sufficiently harmonized, and there involuntarily flowed through

167

Me the great Qualities and Energy of the "Presence" to do the things required in My outer world of activity.

This Good Messenger marveled at the harmony of My men at the ranch and at the mine. That was not because of any outer volition of Mine, but was the result—now please notice this, Beloved Ones—of the Harmony that was maintained within My feeling world. Naturally, the "Presence" saw the opportunity to render a Service through this Harmony which was, as I now know, quite extraordinary.

A love poured forth through My feeling world to all that I contacted. While it seemed quite natural then and took no special effort on My part, yet I know now it was the "Presence" acting—causing a Great Love to flow forth which was of sufficient volume to keep those about Me harmonious. My family, I am so happy to say, never had a discordant vibratory action in their lives. Even Rex and Nada just were obedient. They did not quarrel or seem to have any desire except just the joy and happiness of exercise and freedom. Today there will be many come into the world in that same way.

I want you to know how naturally the Great Law of your "Presence" will act when sufficient Harmony is maintained in your feelings. As I look upon it now, there were many opportunities when I could have felt discordant; but it seemed at every condition that might have started some disturbance, there was always an Inner Action which was stronger.

Now that is your condition, Beloved Ones, today. No matter what the outer provocation is, you, in the Knowledge of your "Presence," have acting—now notice—you have acting a stronger Impulse from your "Presence" which will control you and enable you to feel harmonious in the face of all provocation. This is what I so much want to convey into your feeling world tonight. You actually have Self-control and Mastery in your Acknowledgment of the "Presence."

Do not make it a struggle; just let your "Presence" act. You need not bother about conditions in the Acknowledgment of your "Presence." For instance, if there be qualities within yourself that you do not care to have there longer, just with a great calm serenity say: " 'Mighty I AM Presence,' take out of me that quality and replace it with Your Satisfaction and Perfection." If it be a habit, do the same thing, and the "Presence" will always respond.

If It does not just at the first time you ask, well surely you would not give up and say, "It just could not be done." That would be a great mistake and an injustice to your "Presence," because your "Presence" never fails. You are the decreer for your world. If through your feelings you requalify that which you have set forth into action, well then you will have the same old result which you previously had.

Simply say to all appearances: "You have no more power in my world! I refuse acceptance of every discordant, limiting appearance! 'Mighty I AM Presence,' take charge and fill my world with Your Activity, with Your Directing Intelligence! Release from Your Treasure House my limitless supply of money and whatever I require! Release from Your Great Fountain of Youth my Eternal Perfection and Beauty!" Ladies, and gentlemen also, should all do this if they wish. It is not vanity to wish to be lovely to look upon.

I say to you blessed ones and the blessed young people that are here: it is a great honor to your Wondrous "Presence" to maintain all the Beauty and Perfection you can. There is no limit to what your "Presence" will do for you in that respect. Give your "Presence" the great honor of releasing Its Infinite Supply of every good thing! Give It the great honor of filling you with Its Eternal, Perfect Health, which It holds for you.

Think of it, Beloved Ones! That Great Stream of Energy flowing into your body and anchored within your Heart is *all* Perfection and Power. Just *feel* that Mighty Energy expanding into every cell of your body. See, you could not have ill health; you could not have disturbance of any kind longer in your body if you would just really do that.

Now notice—if you will pardon My reference to My family—up until the Change took place with Mrs.

Rayborn, which really was not illness and I know it now, there never had been one moment's illness in our family. I know today it was because of the harmony maintained in the feelings. It allowed the Pure Energy of the "Presence" to do Its Perfect Work at the time, just naturally.

This is what you are coming to now, Dear Ones, in your Call to the "Presence." Ere long you will find a sufficiently intensified volume of Energy from your "Presence" flowing in and through your body to keep out, or in other words to keep repelled from your human form, every discordant thing; and what a joyous, wonderful thing that is!

I cite this to you tonight for the benefit and blessing of these blessed ones who have started the Activity here, that you and the young people who are being blessed by it, may know what complete Harmony in your activity means. It means success in every single effort of the outer activity; for if your feeling world is harmonious, everyone who touches its radiance will love you, because there is not anything repellent in it.

If there be discordant and ugly feelings in your feeling world, anyone coming near you, whether they be sensitive or not, cannot help but feel that repellent force. Discord is always repellent. Harmony is always attractive and constantly draws all good to you like a great Magnet. That was what made My success in the outer world of activity. I did not make any special effort, so to speak; but I know now, Dear Ones, it was because of the natural Harmony acting within My feeling world, which attracted things to Me—wealth, health, and those who served Me harmoniously and wonderfully.

You know, from the human sense, a mine is about the most difficult place for people to maintain Harmony and Order in the feeling world, because of the old momentum which has been gained in that activity; but there was complete Harmony maintained in our experience. Those men who were, and are still there, would lay down their lives for Me if they thought it were necessary. They do not know of My Ascension yet. They think I am just traveling in foreign lands. Well, it may be foreign, but very beautiful; yet it could hardly be called foreign lands, for in that Great Octave of Life is Our Real Home.

Oh, Beloved Ones, how I long tonight to just lift you all up into Our Octave where you suddenly become aware of all Beauty and Perfection. As the beloved one sang "The Fragrance of the Lily" tonight [Mrs. Rogers over the radio], I thought, oh, how wonderful is the natural Fragrance of those Higher Octaves of Light when from everyone goes forth that Radiance and Fragrance as of some rare flower. Many of you who are still here in human form will begin to radiate that fragrance as of a rare flower, in the

Acknowledgment of your "Presence." You cannot help it.

We do see clearly the progress, advancement, and Expansion of the Light within your Hearts. What a joy, what an encouragement it is to Us to see mankind at last becoming consciously aware of its own dominion. Through it, the individual holds his own Scepter of Power in his hand, wielding It to give him freedom from limitation. Thus he attains his Ascension.

Who could have believed three years before My Ascension, what was to come? I could have no more believed that such a thing was possible than anything in the world. This Good Brother came into My home, and then so shortly after, Saint Germain came in His Tangible Body. On the first visit, We talked for some hours. In His Presence all seemed so natural. There was not a single feeling within Me of questioning, even of the many wonderful things He said to Me.

On that first visit, He said to Me: "My Brother, Mrs. Rayborn is not dead; there is no such thing. I have assisted Her to make the Ascension." I said to Him, "What is that?" He replied, "Do you not believe in the Ascension of Jesus?" "Well," I answered, "I think I do."

Now remember, Beloved Ones, I was not what you would call a church individual; but I always believed in right, justice, and kindliness. However, when He said that to Me—all the time of course, He was pouring His Wondrous Presence and Assistance into and through My being—as He mentioned the various things, all seemed just as natural as could be. There was never a doubt or a question in my mind as He presented the various points of Activity.

We find so many blessed ones today who, when they become aware of the "Mighty I AM Presence," have no doubts or questions. They just know It is true. Every Heart in human form on Earth knows that the Chart of the "Presence" is true and correct. Many times the intellect still dominates enough so it overrules the Heart temporarily and makes the individual have doubts or questioning as to Its Reality. Once any individual has looked upon that Chart, all human doubt and questioning must cease and will disappear because every Heart knows Its own great Reality and Perfection. Every Heart knows that Mighty "Presence" is there, and the opportunity of calling your attention to It is the most wonderful thing which ever could come to mankind anywhere.

When Saint Germain said to Me: "You shall meet Mrs. Rayborn ere long, and it is possible for you to make the Ascension with My Assistance"—can you just feel My feeling now? I just accepted it, never questioning how or anything about it. I just accepted it and like a child I said to Him, "Well, whatever I can do, You can depend on Me, I will do to assist." When we went to the Cave of Symbols and for the first time Mrs. Rayborn came in Her Wondrous Ascended Body, as tangible as our own physical bodies — no happiness, it seemed to Me, ever could excel it in any way.

I want you to feel how real all of this is which Our Blessed, Wondrous Saint Germain has brought to you. We are the living proof of all He has brought to you, even in so short a time. I want you to feel this. In your outer intellect, you do not realize what your "Presence" might do for you in a given time or quickly. I did not know what was to happen, any more than this Good Brother assisting in the Ascension on Mount Shasta, had any idea of what he experienced. That is why We in every way try to convey this into your feeling world; for in no wise, Beloved Ones, limit yourselves or what the "Presence" can do in, through, and for you. Watch out for that, and do not let your human feeling limit you in any way.

Precious Ones, in your Decrees and Songs tonight, considering the number of individuals here, it was simply amazing the Power and Energy that you released. I congratulate you with all My Heart. Never weary in the wondrous work which you are doing here in your Group. We, from time to time, will endeavor to convey to you certain Qualities, certain Activities that you may not just be aware of for the time being. Yet all of a sudden you will find Them coming into outer manifestation in your activity as you go forward.

During this time before the wonderful Class [Pan Pacific Auditorium] there will be a great joy; for really a great preparation is going on within you so that you will comprehend and receive more, perhaps, from this Class than all that have gone before. Does that sound rather incredible? It is not, because as you advance in the Expansion of the Light which illumines the mind, you will find a greater clearness acting—a luminous comprehension, as it were.

Point after point of vital importance, you will grasp like that [quick wave of hand], hold fast to it, and never let it get away—because all these Qualities charged into your feeling world by Us, who are endeavoring so earnestly to give forth the greatest possible Assistance, will always remain active there. It is not an Activity that can ever be lost to you. Thus, a sincere effort is being made before this Class to do this; for We want you blessed ones in Los Angeles, on the return of the Messengers, to be prepared for certain things which We hope to find manifest.

Would you say that this is a Promise? Not quite. Yet who knows? Oh, Beloved Ones, when We have gained such complete Freedom and see the great love and sincerity in the Hearts of those yet in embodiment, do you think there is anything in the world that We would not do which is within the Great Law, to give you Assistance to the same Freedom? Oh, how We long to see you absolutely free, standing with Us.

Tonight there is a marvelous Activity, because of the transformation which is taking place within your Inner feeling world. It is a boundless joy to Me and to Others who are present. Oh, Dear Ones, this is no idle fancy, but a Real and Mighty, Glorious Activity that is going on within you precious ones, to your Complete and Wondrous Freedom! Oh, Blessed Ones, go forward with great, firm determination to have your Freedom and your birthright, to have all that your "Mighty I AM Presence" has held so long in Its Treasure House for you!

While I have this opportunity tonight, I want to say a word to this Good Brother. I know you will not mind our Heart-to-Heart talk. I want him to know that I have not forgotten all that came to Me through him; for had he not come into My home, perhaps all might have been different. Saint Germain—Eternal Blessings be upon Him—knew and brought this Good Brother to Me, as He has brought him to you. To the other Blessed Messenger, you must feel how great is My Gratitude.

Dear Ones, I know this Brother seems so natural and like you. Yet could you see what is constantly going on within his outer garment, you would be surprised. This is why, Dear Ones, We can pour forth such a Radiance to you and into your feeling world, to give you such great Assistance. Somehow tonight I feel that I can say things to you in this respect which I would not have done perhaps otherwise. Therefore, you must know, I feel that We are just like a family discussing the Perfection of Life. Will you not feel that too?

Just with such a great joy, accept into your feeling world your Complete Freedom from all limitations, your absolute Self-control and Mastery over all conditions in your feeling world. Go forth from tonight, glorified by the full consciousness of your Mastery over your world, self, and conditions! May you keep all so perfectly harmonious that there will quickly flood forth from your "Presence," the Purifying Activity which allows the full Dominion of your "Presence" to act at all times. Then you will not need anyone in the world to tell you the joy of having come to know your "Mighty I AM Presence."

We are so Real, Dear Ones! One day, when you come to shake hands and visit with Us in the visible, tangible Body, you will see We are very Real! We are Real Substance. This is what I want you to know: that as you come to the point where you make the Ascension, you take the refined human body with you. There is nothing left behind. As it is raised and absorbed into the Higher Mental Body, the Great Transformation takes place. The Great Ray of Light descends and the finer, purified human form is absorbed into the Higher Mental Body. Then, It ascends into the Electronic Body and you become the Ascended Being, as was My great Joy and Privilege.

You never again after the Ascension come into embodiment as you are today. It is the end of all human pilgrimage on Earth. Then in that great purified, Eternal Light-Body of Substance, you go forward anywhere in the Universe you choose, receiving all Wisdom and Power firsthand. You may call forth anytime, anywhere, all you require to perform any given Service upon the Earth or on any other Planet.

Do you grasp the fullness of this? I hope I will be able to help you do so tonight. Do you grasp how — and what Eternal Freedom the Ascension means? You are not only free from the limitations of Earth, but you can go in your Ascended Body and minister to the people of Earth in such great Power and Activity. You can also go anywhere in the Universe and receive firsthand, through actual experience, any Knowledge or Wisdom that you seek. Then, do you not see how the Ascended Master is the greatest possible Assistance to the Children of Earth? They are almost unknown to mankind. Through the Kumaras, as the Vanguard from Venus, has mankind been sustained throughout all these hundreds of thousands of years — for more than four million years. Yet mankind, after every great height has been reached, has responded to the pull of the human senses; for that pull was still great enough to draw individuals again into limitations.

Is it not an appalling thing to think that mankind could have come into a state where the outer pull of the senses was the controlling force, in spite of this great Infinite Power and Light which beats every Heart? Yet it was so. It has been so up until now when the Great Cosmic Light has come to the Assistance of mankind and is making possible this Achievement.

Does it seem incredible when I say to you tonight that more than two thirds of humanity who become aware of the "Mighty I AM Presence" in this embodiment, will either free themselves in this embodiment or the next? Think of it, Beloved Ones, in comparison with that which has been attained up to this time! The Ascensions have been at most only two a year, even in the Retreats of the World.

Now today, in this Understanding of the "Mighty I AM Presence" which Saint Germain has brought forth, there will be hundreds even in this embodiment who will make the Ascension. Then in the next embodiment there will be thousands who will accomplish it! It is almost an inconceivable thing to the average intellect, which has not been raised into this Consciousness and Understanding of the "Presence," but such is the Truth. Blessed Ones, you have a privilege today that never has been known before on the Earth.

Tonight, in seeing your wonderful, sincere efforts and activity, I was the One chosen to come forth and speak My Heart to you, by flashing these Words before this Good Brother. I feel it a great privilege and joy. Will you accept that which I have endeavored to pour forth into your feeling world? Will you accept the Perfection of your "Mighty I AM Presence," all-powerfully active within you and your outer world of activity, knowing that from this day forth you cannot be deprived of anything which you require for use in your Service of the Light?

I am so grateful for these young people who are here. What a wonderful thing for them to be willing to enter into your closed Group. Do you not see, Beloved Ones, that it is a most amazing thing from the human sense to find such lovely young people willing to do that—to abide by these regulations and requirements? Yet how great, oh, how great will be their reward and blessing!

Oh, Beloved, Blessed Ones, rejoice forever that this Knowledge of the "Mighty I AM Presence" has been brought to you; that you have the privilege of calling Its Mighty Intelligent Energy into action to produce Perfection for you and your world, to make everything harmonious. See, as you go forward in the Expansion of your Light each day, how everything becomes more and more harmonious in and about you as you continue to call your Wondrous "Presence" forth into action. Do you not see, Beloved Ones, there is naught of human creation that can stand before the Onrush of this Mighty Energy which you call forth from the "Presence"? Not a thing that can.

Do not accept anything as longer having power to interfere with It! I plead with you, to all human appearances say with calm firmness: "You have no power! You cannot longer interfere with my world! Stand aside! and let the Glory of my 'Presence' do Its Perfect Work!" Then you will go forward so quickly into the great Eternal Freedom which every Heart knows and craves.

Tonight, in the Infinite Blessing of your "Mighty I AM Presence" and the Great Host of Ascended Masters, I call forth the Perfection of the "Mighty I AM Presence" of each one of you, into full command and action in your Life and world—to hold Its Dominion in mind and body, to produce Its Perfection there, to quickly expand the Light within your Heart until Its All-powerful Radiance fills you and your world, that every impurity and imperfection be swept out of your mind, body, world, and activity! Then you stand glorified, the "Mighty I AM Presence" in action.

Mrs. Rayborn, Rex, Nada, Bob, and Pearl all join Me in pouring forth Their Love to you, and Their full Consciousness of your Victory and Freedom. As you go forward, remember, We shall always stand by to give every Assistance that is possible for your Complete Freedom from everything that has bound you in the outer world. Be firm! Be determined! Yield not an inch to human appearances! And as you withdraw from them all power, then in the full Power of your "Presence," remember: God, the "Mighty I AM Presence" which beats your Heart, is your certain Victory! I thank you.

META'S DISCOURSE

BELOVED Children whose Home is in the Light, We reach forth Our Loving Arms to hold you in Our Embrace of Light, in your conscious endeavor to free yourselves from human creation and limitation. Well do I know what that means, and what Happiness is in store for you as in your great firm determination you continue to call for the Great Loving, Powerful Activity of your "Mighty I AM Presence" to flood your mind, body, and world, and do for you that which your "Presence" alone is able to accomplish. Then in every effort that you make, you find in that achievement a permanently attained and established activity; for you do not have to keep repeating it, because once accomplished, it stands there serving you.

You who are having this Knowledge of the "Presence," your "Mighty I AM," are fortunate above all children of Earth. You become a *Great Golden Sun* as well, for you have an All-powerful Scepter of Dominion within your grasp to use. Any one of you

184

children from four, five, or six years can and will begin to use that Scepter with definite precision. This means the gaining of a momentum and achievement which is dauntless before all mankind.

We, all of Us who have reached the Ascended State, Beloved Ones, have gone identically the same way. There is but one road to the Eternal Perfection and Freedom for mankind! It is this identical Knowledge of the "Presence" which Saint Germain has brought forth. There is no other road in all the Universe. Every one of Us had to follow these same Steps which He has brought to you, so simplified.

In Our time the attainment was far more complicated than the Application you have today in the outer experience. Yet in that Great Simplicity, those Great Ones from Venus assisted in bringing It forth. May I remind you who are here tonight of the statement of the Great Master from Venus, when the arrangement was made for these Books to go forth? He said emphatically that these Books must go forth in a simple language which the layman could understand —free from all technical terms; and the Great Wisdom of His Decree has in thousands of ways been made manifest already. Even the children are able to apply this Law, quite as well as the grown people, and with quite as firm, definite results. That proves the Ascended Masters' Wisdom which brought forth the "I AM" Instruction in this simplicity. It is free from all old terminology which has been so confusing to mankind in the various things that have come forth before, because each in itself has had different terminology.

Observe the people of India and Persia where We gained Our Victory — of the Orient, of the various parts of the World! Never — anywhere — has this Great Knowledge come forth so simplified and so purified as Saint Germain has given It to you. Any human being on the face of the Earth who will earnestly with determination apply these Laws according to the Direction He has given, and put out of the mind all previous concepts, will have such magnificent results as no one on the Earth could imagine, until he tries it out.

Tonight it is My Great Joy while I am talking to you — and that is Our reason for coming forth in the Groups — to pour forth Our Radiance and Closeness. It is just as though We took each one of you individually in Our Arms in the physical form and held you close, that you might know how REAL We are. One day you will know there is nothing intangible about Us.

You mothers and fathers! I am a Mother of three Children. The Master Cha Ara, who dictated to you recently, is My son, and there are two other Children who are not known in the outer world, as He is. The three Children did not make their Ascension until after I did, but all of Our family did make the Ascension. As soon as I had made Mine, I was able to render Assistance to Them; and their willing obedience enabled Them to quickly win the Ascension after My Achievement.

Therefore, Dear Ones, when We speak to you in this manner, you cannot help but feel Our Reality and the Truth of which We speak, because It is the Truth—and your Heart knows the Truth in spite of your intellect. This is the thing, Precious Ones, that every earnest "I AM" Student will come to understand so very vividly. It is why this Good Messenger has said to the Class so many times: "Anyone without a spark of Faith, who will with earnest sincerity begin to call the 'Mighty I AM Presence' into action, will have all the proof in the world he wants—which will give him Faith if he does not have It already." This is a most astounding Statement to make, but it is true. The World has tried to live on Faith without Understanding. Its supply appears sometimes and sometimes it does not.

This is what has distressed mankind so greatly because in prayer as the orthodox world has known of it, sometimes the feeling was intensely poured forth in the prayer, which released the Power of the "Presence" to fulfill it, but not always. There have been a great many prayers that have not been answered. Now in your Knowledge and Call to the "Mighty I AM

Presence," which is the greatest Power in the Universe, you cannot fail to have an Answer. Stand by your "Presence," which is your Life, and know this Ascended Master Understanding, Beloved Ones! It does not require Faith! You have the Understanding which knows where the Powerhouse is — the Intelligence — and knows positively that you are really a part of It. It being anchored within you, within your Heart, then you know you have Its Authority there. Not even your intellect can interfere with your earnest Call, if you will make the Call!

If you will hold fast to this, you will find there will never be a single failure in your entire experience through your Call to the "Presence." You must know by this time that your Heart is a part of your "Mighty I AM Presence" anchored within, acting within your human form — which knows all the Perfection there is. You have your Higher Mental Body which is your Selective, Discriminating Intelligence. It is only too delighted to release from the "Presence" everything you require. It knows exactly what you require for any given purpose. When We came to know that, and after We had made earnest Application, We began to find that We were actually speaking to the "Presence," and often audibly.

We found We could receive Its Instruction direct. We found that a certain Intimation would be given. Then We would release certain Currents of Energy, and They would do certain things in Our forms. Then We found that by a Great Flood of Light from the "Presence," We could sweep out of Our minds and bodies every discordant thing. Always in the beginning of the Awakening of the people to this, is the use of the Violet Consuming Flame given to them through which, if they be determined and sincere, they can purify and consume all their previous human accumulation. If used earnestly and sincerely with determination for a short time, it does not take years to enable you to be free.

Beloved Ones, if you are earnest enough, you will use this Violet Consuming Flame to dissolve and consume every bit of discordant creation which has been drawn about you throughout the centuries. That is the Magnificent Mercy of the "Presence" to mankind today. No matter how great the mistakes have been, by the constant use of the Violet Consuming Flame you can dissolve and consume every discordant thing which you have drawn into your world through the centuries. Beloved Ones, this is what We are trying so earnestly to convey into your feeling world. It does not require long periods of time to do this. If you will do it earnestly, you will feel the results in yourself, a lightness in your human forms, and a freedom which will prove your accomplishment to you in the use of the Violet Consuming Flame.

Now Beloved Ones, this is the first Fundamental

Activity. As you use the Violet Consuming Flame, it causes the "Presence" to set It into action and keeps It sustained when your mind is on something else. The Violet Consuming Flame acts! You do have to set aside a few moments several times a day while you are accepting Its Activity. Call the "Presence" to sustain Its Activity and keep It going on all the time, until every particle of your discordant accumulation of the centuries is dissolved and consumed.

In this way, Dear Hearts, you can so quickly free yourselves. I plead with you, Precious Ones, call your "Mighty I AM Presence" into action to do this with great Power and Speed that you may be free. (You will pardon Me, Lady Betty, if I talk too fast.) Dear Ones, you can accomplish anything that your Hearts desire for your freedom in this Acknowledgment of the "Presence." Do not let anything cause you to feel otherwise!

Now remember, Precious Ones, you must stand guard over your world! With the use of the Violet Consuming Flame and the Tube of Light, which you have learned to draw forth into action, you make yourselves invincible to the further discord of the outer world. Thus, as the Violet Consuming Flame consumes all that has been drawn into your world, you stand free! Then when you call your "Mighty I AM Presence" into action, Its Power can release with perhaps twenty, thirty, or forty times more speed than It does before you use the Violet Consuming Flame enough to dissolve the human accumulation which has been drawn about you. You do not know in the outer what is there, and it is not necessary to know. Fortunately for you, you do not; but when you call the "Presence" into action to consume your human accumulation, it is done completely. Then you will never have to look upon it.

We have called to the Divine Director and those directly in charge of that Activity, to impel you so earnestly and powerfully to do this so you will never have to look upon any single part of your human, discordant creation. If you once knew the Mercy which the use of the Violet Consuming Flame is to mankind, you would sing Praises forever. In those earlier centuries, the Students never attained without looking upon some of their own human creation, and it was a most unhappy thing. We had to do it. Having discovered the way to avoid it, do you wonder We plead with mankind to believe Us and prove Us, that they may avoid many difficult things which We had to go through in Our Attainment and Achievement?

In the beginning of Our Freedom, the great paramount idea was to maintain Life in the body over long periods of time. I had maintained Youth and Perfection in My Body for more than five hundred years before I made the Ascension. My son Cha Ara had maintained Youth and Perfection in His Body for more than three hundred years before His Ascension. In those earlier centuries the great paramount idea was to be able to do that. Today among mankind, in one great sweeping activity in the Acknowledgment of the "Presence," the individual goes forth into his Eternal Freedom, Victory, and Ascension with a speed almost inconceivable, compared to the time the Beloved Lady Master Nada made Her Ascension.

Oh, Dear, Precious Ones, We want so earnestly to convey to you the Privilege which you have today, transcendent beyond anything that has ever been known in the World. We have worked for hundreds of years, waiting for the time when this could be brought forth to mankind, that the great mass of mankind could understand It. Oh, I am sure you all appreciate how magnificent and wonderful It is. That there is a single one of mankind today who is not yet ready to accept this great magnificent simplicity and Freedom which is brought forth to them, seems incredible. In the Patience of waiting hundreds of years for this point, a few months or few years ought to be easy to wait for the rest of mankind to suddenly awaken to their "Mighty I AM Presence," and have Its Freedom and Blessing which this brings.

Now Dear Ones, will you not be more and more

in earnest and determined every day? I think of that day so long ago, as you think of time, when My Children were like these. It was quickly, even in that time, under Our Instruction and Direction that They were able to set Themselves Free. It is true, in the outer world at that time They perhaps did not have as much charged into the atmosphere about Them as the children do today, because We were in a far less densely populated part of the country.

Dear Ones, in a day not far distant, mankind will learn to live again in homes — not in buildings where hundreds of people live in one building. Where one or two individuals live in a building which is charged with discord, those persons necessarily have a battle to hold their own atmosphere free from that charge of discordant limitation about them. However, this is the Truth, if one chose to make the effort: You may take a twenty-apartment building and one family in it could begin filling the building with absolute Harmony and Happiness. They could hold it there, just for the joy of calling the "Presence" into action, to prove for themselves that they could do it. Even people without understanding would respond to the feeling with which the building would be charged.

This is why, Precious Ones, We ask you and the Messengers have asked you almost from the beginning, not to let one morning pass that you do not raise your hands to the "Presence" and, just like you reached into the Great Substance of Light from the Ascended Masters' Octave of Life, charge the walls of the room with this Pure Substance of the "Mighty I AM Presence." Charge It to be sustained and continually pour forth that Purifying, Harmonious Radiance to everyone who enters. Beloved Ones, if you would only do that!

These precious ones [Mr. and Mrs. David Lucas] have been doing that in the school, until the Radiance is wonderful and beautiful. We love to give Assistance by amplifying every sincere effort of that kind. Therefore, you can make the atmosphere wonderful through just charging, so everyone who enters and touches it feels the Harmony and Freedom all about him, where discord was just a few moments before.

You know it is so easy to forget discord, if you only will; but it is not so easy if you do not want to. You have Free Will, Precious Ones — do not forget it! You are the decreer for your world, your business, and your activity! What you decree for yourself, your business, your home, must come forth if you do not allow it to be interrupted by discord in your own feelings. It is a Law, the Great Law of Life, Precious Ones. Oh, once the Students of the "I AM" begin to realize and understand that whatever they fix their attention on which is constructive, will be successful, will bring in supply of all required for their happiness and comfort, will give them abundance of all they wish to give in Service to the Light!

I want you to feel tonight, oh, Our Great Closeness — the Great Reality of the Ascended Masters, the Legion of Light, and the Great Cosmic Beings, who are now sweeping the Great Cosmic Light into the Earth. Feel how close and how real It is! You have become a part of It! Do not let anything cause you to feel longer that you are not a part of this Great Cosmic Light which is filling the Earth. Besides your Call to your own "Presence," glorify the Assistance of this Great Cosmic Light. Why?

I do not recall that you have had this particular point explained to you, but tonight let Us take it up definitely. Why, besides your Call to the "Mighty I AM Presence," are you receiving a definite and powerful Assistance from the Great Cosmic Light which is flooding the Earth? Because your own Light within your Heart is a Magnet for the drawing of this Great Cosmic Light to you at your point in the Universe. Then do you not see how again it is the Great Beneficent Law that is assisting you without limit? Surely, you must understand and comprehend how great is your ability in that respect.

I repeat again and again and again to you: Never in the history of the World has such an Opportunity been offered mankind! You are receiving — oh,

Precious Ones, brought to you in the comfort of your own homes, so to speak — that Knowledge which human beings a few centuries ago traveled over the Earth hundreds of miles on foot to reach. Do you realize, Precious Ones, how before and after Jesus' ministry, mankind made pilgrimages everywhere, to try to make contact with those who knew the Law. Yet in those very days there was only a fragment of this Law given into the outer world, which you have today as a Free Gift of Love.

I want you tonight, if I may help you, to realize fully the marvelous Blessing that is at your door, which has entered into your world — for you are no longer subject to any limitations through any mistakes which you have made. Feel that for a moment deeply. You are not subject longer to any limitations, no matter what your mistakes have been. If you will earnestly call on the Law of Forgiveness, call the use of the Violet Consuming Flame into action, call the "Presence" to place about you the Tube of Light, then you have fulfilled the Requirements. You have fulfilled the Requirements of the Great Law; and the Great Law, which is "the Light of God that never fails," must respond to you — Its own. You are not separate, Beloved Ones, from the Life which beats your Heart.

Remind yourself of this often. Sometimes, when something of human discord touches you from without, draw yourself up; straighten your spine; and say with great calm serenity: "Stop this nonsense! 'Mighty I AM Presence,' You are in command here! Silence every human thing! Take command and direct me by Your Mighty Intelligence! See that I do not make a single mistake! See that my human gives obedience in every way." Then, you set the Great Law into Action—Precious Ones, the Law of the Universe in Action, your Law of Life—to produce what you require, and It cannot fail!

This is why, Beloved Children, I want you to know that you too can produce the same wonderful activity in your Life which We have. Before five years are over your heads you can have your Life so filled with harmony and happiness that everyone who touches you will love you. Everywhere you move, all will love to serve you; and even the grown-ups can do that, if they will! As you call your Mighty "Presence" into action, people will love to serve; for that is where Divinity enters into the activity of the Earth. Think! within the natural life-span of these precious children here there will come such Perfection into this World as you could scarcely conceive, even today.

Remember, Precious Ones, the Great Cosmic Law makes no mistakes! When this Beloved Messenger saw upon the Great Cosmic Screen seventy years of the future of America, those Great Ascended Masters make no mistakes! In this great Call to the

"Mighty I AM Presence" and the Great Host of Ascended Masters to take command of America and the World, do not be dismayed when human, discordant appearances continue to find expression for a time. Do not be dismayed; but go on and on and on, calling your "Mighty I AM Presence" into Action to take command of America, Its people, and Its activities, to produce Perfection and hold Its Dominion forever. Thus, as We go forth in the mental and feeling world of mankind everywhere, soon thousands and thousands will take up that Mighty Decree and compel Perfection to be the Directing Intelligence of our government—your government—and bless the Earth with It!

Please remember, when the Mighty Arcturus said: "If it be necessary for the Protection of mankind, that Light as of a Thousand Suns will descend into the Earth, dissolve and consume all human discord and selfishness from the Planet," He knew whereof He spoke. Mankind must be preserved until the power of the Incoming Golden Age can find Its full Dominion; for the Earth must become the Light which the Great Cosmic Law has decreed. It must expand the Light and send It forth!

It is no longer a matter of human requirements or activity; but the Great Cosmic Light has said, "The Earth must blaze forth more Light!"—and so it shall be! All those who will cooperate with that Great Law will find such Expansion of their Light that no longer will they be aware of any discordant thing. They will move in the world untouched by human discord. As they pour forth the Great Radiance of Love from their "Mighty I AM Presence," It becomes so powerful that nothing else can come in. They then move in the world untouched by discord, pouring forth their Light and Love everywhere, until all are free.

See how great your privilege is, oh Precious Ones, not only in having your own freedom, but in the Blessing you can pour forth to the rest of mankind, who are struggling, struggling, struggling. Oh, Precious Ones, you know what your own struggles have been — all so unnecessary — just because you had forgotten and did not understand any longer. Will you not enter with great and full joy into this Freedom which is yours now, and be the Perfection of your "Mighty I AM Presence," constantly called forth into action by you?

Now Beloved Ones, remember: Besides these two Activities of calling your "Presence" into action and the Assistance of the Great Cosmic Light, around your "Mighty I AM Presence," as shown by the Circle of Color on the Chart, is your own Accumulation of Good, which the "Presence" has drawn there and holds for you. It is your Accumulation of Good through the centuries. Once you have given

sufficient attention to your "Mighty I AM Presence,"
then that Good will be released into your outer use;
for It is the threefold Activity of the Mighty Unfed
Flame — the most powerful Activity which can be given
into the use of the Children of Earth.

One day, possibly in three places in your America,
will stand visible to all, that Mighty Unfed Flame!
Then you will not require human laws in your land
to hold all in Obedience; but because of the Great
Light within themselves, all will give natural and willing Obedience — as they did in the civilization in South
America referred to as the Buried Cities of the Amazon,
as they did in the seventy-thousand-year civilization
in which Saint Germain was the Ruler. All of that
great Perfection will come again, on even a spiral
higher in Its Great Perfection. This time It is to be
eternally sustained.

So you of today are living in a period and have a
Privilege unparalleled on Earth. Will you not keep
yourselves reminded of this? For your precious children, will you not call their "Mighty I AM Presence"
to take command of each mind and body, produce
Its Perfection and hold Its Dominion there, filling
their lives with the Beauty and Perfection which the
"Presence" holds for them? No matter what the provocation, hold your own feelings always harmonious.
Then see how quickly your homes, your lives will be
filled with the Glory of your "Presence," which is

Divine Love in Action and pours out through all concerned into your world and all that touches it.

My Precious Ones, may I just take a few moments longer to call your attention to an activity that We have seen manifest through the Messengers. In various places they have been, such inharmony and confusion reigned; but just as quickly as they came, all that subsided and disappeared. You in Los Angeles at one time saw the activity of just such great chaos. You saw when they returned how quickly it dissolved and disappeared. It can be so in your individual Life —just the same. The "Presence" did it then; the "Presence" will do it individually. When the Blessed Ones went to San Francisco, confusion was reigning there through unfortunate individuals who intruded themselves. Again, wonderful Blessing and Happiness reigns. So it is everywhere. Any place there is one or more who can stand firm and unyielding in the Activity of their "Mighty I AM Presence," Its Radiance goes forth without limit and performs Its Miracles of Harmonious Activity. This is what I want you to feel, if you will: that you too are a Pillar of Light moving in your world, whose Radiance from the "Presence" is so strong that no discord can exist in the world about you. As you determine, decree and feel this, so does it come about and cause it to be eternally sustained. It is a beautiful thing! It is within the reach of every precious one of you.

One time about thirty years ago, as you comprehend time, it was My Privilege in India to come upon a condition where a little child had been badly injured. The spine and back had been broken, and one arm and one leg. That little child—a little boy—lay there is such agony, when from the Higher Octaves My attention was called to it. I afterwards found it was because of previous association. I went immediately and lowered the rate of vibration of My Body. I became Visible, just touched the brow of the little child, and immediately all was perfect. Such is the Freedom which your Life can give you! That is the Power without limit which all can wield! As described in *The Magic Presence,* when Saint Germain touched the child that was so distorted—almost beyond recognition—immediately Perfection took its place. So you, or your "Mighty I AM Presence" through you, could today perform a similar Service, if you could but realize it and still your human activity and feeling enough.

Just as through this body you see standing before you here was given such assistance as was recorded in the Books, so could your "Mighty I AM Presence" render a similar Assistance through you. That is what he so earnestly tries to convey to you. Your "Presence" is not limited in what It can do in, for, and through you; but It does require your continued Harmony long enough to let Its Power gain Dominion. Will you not feel that? Keep this before your outer consciousness so you may have the Blessing, Freedom, and Glory of that Light ever manifesting Its Perfection in and through you.

You are no longer limited, Precious Ones! Do not let fear beset you any longer through your seeming lack of finances. Your "Mighty I AM Presence" is your Treasure House; and if you will call earnestly, It will open ways and means by which you are supplied continually. There is no limit to what It wishes you to have. It only asks you to be harmonious long enough so It can pour forth and release all you require.

Precious Ones, think! There are but three things in the world which really deprive mankind of a flood of every good thing; and they are criticism, condemnation, and judgment. That is the origin of almost all the distress of mankind. How easily it could all be stopped and dissolved! The marvel of it is that you may call on the Law of Forgiveness and set the Law into Action to dissolve all mistakes. Do you not see how the full Scepter of Power is in your hands for your Freedom?

Today We offer Our Gift of Love to you and to these blessed ones [Mr. and Mrs. Lucas]. May your "Mighty I AM Presence" fill you and your world with limitless happiness, joy, such release of all the money and of every good thing you require. May It give you limitless Assistance in this Service which you are rendering, and to all who are assisting. May the Glory of Its limitless Supply be released to everyone. May a limitless supply of money be released to carry on this Wonderful Work—the School of the "I AM."

If you will make the Call earnestly and sincerely, then We will endeavor to help you bring the Release of all the money required to carry on as the expansion is needed—to bring about beautiful and perfect places which will be a blessing and a credit to all, to bring limitless blessings for everyone who wishes to help and bless in this work. Remember, you cannot be limited in your Service of the Light, for money or anything else. As you make the Call for it, so will the "Presence" open the way and fulfill It without limit. Try to feel this with wonderful, definite power, and then that Answer will come to you.

We rejoice greatly in the courage and strength many of you have had to step forward and start this. What a wonderful thing! "Where there is a will, there is a way." Remember, your outer determination is the Activity of the Inner Will of your "Mighty I AM Presence." We have referred to this quite often, but We must anchor it within your feelings. When you determine to do a constructive thing, it is the impelling Power of your "Mighty I AM Presence," your Inner Self, not only urging you forward, but It will bring the supply of all that is required to keep it in harmonious action and accomplishment, if you can but realize it and *feel* it.

So with all My Heart I bless you — every one — who have been a part in starting this Activity. Never fear, your "Presence" will sustain and carry you forward into greater and greater expansion, until all the children throughout the Earth may know the "Mighty I AM Presence." Let Me add this, Beloved Ones:

The first Fundamental in all education in the World is the Understanding of the "Mighty I AM Presence." Then all outer phases of education must become easy for the children. As you call the "Mighty I AM Presence" into action to produce Perfection in your educational world, so will the right activity of that education come forth also. All that is of real benefit, will be brought forth through your Call. The needs of the day will be fulfilled in Perfect Divine Order. It is not the thing to do to put your education before your "I AM Presence." Put your "I AM Presence" first! Then the remainder of the education of mankind will follow in Perfect Divine Order. It must be so. You should know that is the Fundamental.

The "right education" does not mean some unusual manner of teaching. It means to know your "Mighty I AM Presence" first, and It will bring about the Perfect Order of the educational system you want to use, as a natural sequence; and it will always be in Divine Order. Wherever inharmony or confusion starts, you will always know there is something in that activity which does not belong in your education. So We want you to know you are entering into the Great Pathway of Life, which is the Balance between religion and education — your "Mighty I AM Presence." I thank you.

DAVID LLOYD'S DISCOURSE

RATANA'S GLENDALE GROUP — GLENDALE, CALIFORNIA

MARCH 24, 1937

OUT of the fullness of My Heart, O Beloved Students of Los Angeles, I send to you on the Words of My Love, the Truth that has given Me My Freedom. Only such a short time ago I, like yourselves, was making My great earnest search for Light and Freedom.

When the Blessed Master in India said to Me, "On a great mountain in North America, you will meet the one who will assist you to the Ascension," I was just a lad; but I believed every word He said. There never was a question in My mind, either in the outer or Inner activity, that ever doubted. Yet, years after My mother passed on, then I began the search.

It seemed incredible, when I went forth with such fragmentary information, that I should attempt to find the mountain, let alone the individual. Yet always there was the Inner Impelling Force which drove Me on. When time after time I met disappointment and I would think to Myself, "I shall give it up," within an hour there would come from within

207

Me a great powerful, Inner Surge which could not be denied, and again I would go forth. Then the day came when, in the joy I had in hiking about on Mount Shasta and at perhaps the least expected time, I came upon this Beloved Brother seated on a log. When the Great Revelation came and I suddenly saw in his hand the Crystal Cup of which the Master had spoken, it seemed all the Powers of My Being—My entire Being—were released.

I did not know up to that moment it was possible to experience such calm joy. Instead of an ecstatic, almost terrifying joy, deep from somewhere within Me came a great deep Joy of knowing. This Good Brother, in astonishment as great as Mine, stood looking at the Cup in his hand. It filled with a Wondrous Liquid, that Wondrous Substance!

Having lived all those years without a single doubt in My being of the ultimate Victory, even at the times when discouragement came, still there always continued a certainty of knowing My Final Victory. I seized and drank that Liquid with great eagerness! Then for a moment I was almost terrified because of the great Electrical Force which charged through every atom of My being. Then the Great Light spread over this form before you, making the arms such blazing Light you could scarcely look into them. Those hands took mine and I felt again a Tremendous Charge flood My being. Each moment the sense of weight grew less. Then as My feet left the Earth, I knew, oh, I knew My Victory had come!

As I speak to you, will each of you beloved ones feel the Truth, feel My Feeling enter into your being? As I describe to you in My humble way that which occurred, so you may have anchored within you My Feeling of the Truth of the Victory, then one day you too shall experience the same thing.

I felt all the density released from My human form and felt the purified part of My human form Ascending. As My hands left his and I continued to stand there in midair, can you imagine the feeling which one would have while standing in midair, just as firmly as you stand upon the floor—not feeling anything but the Goal that was being accomplished?

When you have revolved within your feeling world with great intensity over a period of years, the Glory of the Ascension which had been brought to your attention—as some intimation of Its Activity begins to work in you and your world, you will find there is not a single feeling of anything but just rejoicing in Its Accomplishment.

There will be no human fears, doubts, or analyzing of how you are standing in midair. All those silly human things that confuse so many of mankind are just gone. It is all so simple, Dear Ones. There is nothing complicated about these Transcendent Activities which mankind has now come to understand

—not a single thing confusing or complicated about it. Each one of the Messengers has endeavored to convey the simplicity, the Majesty of this Understanding of the "Mighty I AM Presence," which one day is your Freedom and your Ascension.

Please feel tonight as I am giving you My own Experience, speaking to you the Words of the Truth that actually occurred in My own Life and experience, then you can feel the great Reality of It which will be of untold assistance to you.

I said to this Good Brother as I stood there in midair, Myself not the slightest concerned in consciousness as to what was going to take place, but accepting the Great Wisdom that I knew was acting, "One day I shall return and render you a Service." Tonight, if you will permit Me, I shall render you a Service. Only when you have accomplished the Victory of the Ascension will you see just how much is accomplished in this short hour.

The Transformation took place and I felt it very clearly, but not having a mirror I did not see the Transformation as this Good Brother did. I knew that he was seeing It just as clearly as could be. Then, the Great Ray of Light descended from the "Presence" and I disappeared within It, leaving forever all limitations behind. You just must feel now how I felt then and have felt ever since. It is a Joy too great to try to voice, because It is alone comprehended in the feeling.

I was an Englishman by birth, so grateful for this opportunity—and Englishmen are not any too receptive. Yet how ready I was so to comprehend. Oh, My Dear Ones, in all the wide world there is nothing that really matters but Freedom from human limitations and your Ascension. Then in one day you can serve almost as much as one lifetime in the physical form.

Now will you rejoice with Me that tonight My Service has begun in the outer world again. You cannot imagine—I am sure you cannot—My Joy. You love the Beloved Messengers, I know; but you can hardly compare your love with My Love to this Good Brother through whom My Victory was made possible. It is difficult for the outer intellect to comprehend, Precious Ones, just what that means; but I assure you, through My Feeling I shall endeavor with all earnestness to convey My Feeling into your feeling world, and qualify It to act there with definite power and purpose for you.

Do not ever let your human say to you these things are imagination, or they are not true. What a pity anyone in the world could ever for a moment have such a feeling. We speak to you from the Ascended State and flash these Words, Our Words, before this Good Brother. No human concept can enter.

Do you think from the Ascended Master Octave an untruth could be uttered? If you think that, then you know very little of the Great Law. It is the same

when one is passing through the change called death
—an untruth cannot be spoken! From the Ascended
Masters' Octave of Life no untruth dare be spoken!
There is no one who could ever have a desire to speak
an untruth.

So today the greatest possible Blessing has come to
you precious ones who have been drawn under the Radiation of the Beloved Saint Germain. To Him is due
all credit for this Knowledge coming forth to mankind. All of the Ascended Masters acknowledge it.
How all love Him, no words could possibly tell you;
for the Love of the "Mighty I AM Presence" transcends
anything that you have yet understood in your world
of human love. Why do I say "human love"? Because,
Dear Hearts, until you have made the Ascension, there
is always some more or less human qualification acting within your love. It could not be otherwise, for
only as you come to the final preparation is all human love replaced by the Transcendent Love of the
"Presence." In your understanding of the "Presence"
today, you can still the outer human emotion which
would requalify the Love from the "Presence," until
the Great Divine Love of the "Presence" can flow
forth, scarcely touched by your human qualification
which many times qualifies the Love of the "Presence"
into what we call human love.

There is no human, except the discordant creation
which mankind has generated. Your forms that you

call human are but a clothing of density. It is all that can be human. Your Divine Pattern, your Light Pattern within you, is not human. Just the quality is human, which you have imposed upon your Light Pattern by discordant feeling. You have come to know this very definitely. Today you realize that, and know how harmony maintained in your feeling will enable the Power of Pure Energy, the Love from your "Presence," to flow through and out into your world. Then you begin to become a Divine Being.

Notice, Beloved Ones, in the Experience of Mr. Rayborn and Myself, how all this, when it came to the Final Activity, was done very quickly. Now, you are understanding this Wondrous Knowledge of the "Mighty I AM Presence," as you are constantly and earnestly calling It into action. While your purification and accomplishment is going on, you are rendering a tremendous Service to everyone you contact, because if your desire is very intense for your Freedom and Ascension, then you pour out that feeling naturally.

Your Higher Mental Body, which knows all requirements, will utilize every opportunity to intensify your feeling—not only for yourself, but for all who come into the Radiance of your world and activity. Therefore, you are always rendering a threefold service in your great intense desire for your Freedom and Ascension.

When I saw from the unlimited state what every step gained in the Acknowledgment of the "Presence" meant, I thought no words could ever express My Gratitude. Oh, that all mankind could suddenly grasp this one simple point! What transformations would take place! Once blessed mankind realizes that the power of qualification alone has been the stumbling block in the road to Perfection, all individuals can discontinue qualifying any activity with discord.

They can hold all human activity in obedience to their great Call. They can release from the "Presence" this Wondrous Energy — Self-luminous, Intelligent Substance which will replace all imperfection (as it is taken out of every cell of the human form) by this Pure Substance, the Ascended Master Substance which the human cannot requalify. Will you not think deeply upon this?

Think of this one simple point alone: the privilege mankind has today that the Great Host of Ascended Masters and Cosmic Beings have provided for you to bless you, in the use of this Ascended Master Substance which cannot be requalified by the human. If the blessed, precious Students would understand this, oh, how rapid would be the change and transformation within their bodies and activity, because then they would keep charging the Ascended Master Substance into their minds and bodies and out into their worlds and activity.

Ere long the Creative Power of the Ascended Master Substance and Consciousness, which contains within It no discord, would begin to act in full Power in their worlds. Then all human struggle would cease. Do you not see this, Beloved Ones, how quickly all human struggle would cease?

Then let this great calm Serenity and Substance enter into your feeling world; and through It, let everything in your emotional world become so still that nothing can agitate it. You know, if you take a spoon in a jar of liquid and begin to stir it rapidly, how agitated it becomes? Well, that is the condition of most emotional bodies during, shall We say, the greater part of the day. The moment you touch some discord, your emotional body begins to vibrate just like that [quick motion of hand] to the extent that sometimes you think you have Heart trouble.

Think what it means to come to a point, Precious Ones, where all disturbing vibration is perfectly still and quiet. In all your former understanding, "that Peace that passeth understanding" is really this Great Inner Stillness. In the Acknowledgment of your "Presence," you come to the point as this Good Brother has, when such great, great Calmness becomes like the deep still waters where there is no longer agitation and disturbance. Then one has to be very firm against touching the discord of the outer world.

May I call this to your attention tonight, O Beloved Ones, so you realize what it means for a human form to be in the Powerful Vibratory Action of the Ascended Beings in the various Dictations which have taken place in your midst here during the week? Last Sunday, three Great Beings dictated and flashed Their Words before him. He must be in Their Radiation while that is being done. Then, can you imagine what the touch of a little discord of the outer world means? You would never hear him complain or say a word; but I tell you this, that you might know what it means when discord touches his world when he is raised to that Height. I want you to know, because We love him so greatly. I know you do also, but I want you to know the Great Laws that are acting.

His outer garment is like yours, Beloved Ones, but not the Inner. I ask the Staff and those immediately about him — will you not do everything in your power to hold the greatest harmony possible, as this greater Expansion and greater Power is released to bless the Students everywhere? He is steadily, as is Mrs. Ballard, steadily raising in Attunement. Your great love that pours out to them is the most wonderful thing, Beloved Ones. If individuals who are unkind and pour out criticism, condemnation, and judgment to them could see what they do, they would not do it the second time.

They, who pour forth only such great love and kindness, have sacrificed everything of the human world—if you call it a sacrifice—to carry forth this Message of Light, Love, and Truth. Precious Ones, do not let the silly human reports go forth which have been spread at times that they are flourishing with money. All they have is the Love Gifts of the Students to carry on the Work. Not so long ago the report went forth that they had plenty of money. The Love Gifts from that Class did not take care of the express on their trunks, but they never complain.

So I want you to know this, Dear Hearts. Fortify yourselves against the foolish human gossip which would try to bring discredit upon these Loved Ones whom the Great Ones love so greatly. They have had the courage to go forth and carry this Light with never a thought of themselves; but because they knew the Knowledge was so great and the Freedom so certain for mankind, they have been courageous to carry It forward. They will continue until the great mass of mankind understands that they themselves have become the Guardians of this Light.

Today, Precious Ones, Blessed Students of Los Angeles and southern California, you have become the Guardians of the Light. Remember that! Feel this is your part of the problem. If you are not strong enough, but listen to human, foolish, silly gossip which turns you aside from this Great Truth—the Mightiest ever brought forth on Earth—then you must pay the penalty by failure. One said, who came to this Good Brother today, that certain individuals had said, well, they thought they were not interested any more in this Truth. Beloved Ones, how can human beings be so foolish! They can no more turn away from their "Mighty I AM Presence" than they can sprout wings and fly this very moment. They may temporarily turn aside; but only too glad will they be to turn back to this Mighty Source of Life, their "Mighty I AM Presence."

Oh, Precious Ones, do you not see it is not a matter of the Messengers saying that this Knowledge of the "Mighty I AM Presence" is true; but everyone has a "Presence" of his own, which should tell him that somewhere there is a Source of Life—Individualized—which gives him Life and activity! It is not contained in the human form at death; every one of you knows that. Every organ or faculty is in your body, but it is of no use. Then the Stream of Life which has been pouring into the body must have withdrawn somewhere. Remember! You are here! Then you must know that the "Presence" is there, or you would not be here!

Tonight, oh, Beloved Ones, My Joy is so great for the privilege of speaking My Wishes, My Experiences to you; for only so short a time ago I stood where you are today. This is not a far-off thing, Dear Hearts. It is such a recent Experience that It should touch your Hearts and feeling world. Qualify It with your conscious, certain knowledge that if I could accomplish It, then you can too. Do you not see how all this is an Example to the outer world? It is an Infinite, definite, All-powerful Truth and Reality! It is an Example to you that you should attain your Freedom and Ascension without question.

Blessed, Beloved Ones, no words can describe Our Love for you and the great Desire which pours forth without limit into your feeling world, to assist you unto a like Accomplishment. I know now—so far as financial supply was concerned—I was provided for, while all this great search went on. Through the kindness of My father, who grubstaked a man in the diamond fields in South Africa, the Great Law provided for Me.

Precious Ones of today, oh, do not, please do not ever allow your human self to make you feel once again that you can be deprived of the money you desire for your happiness, comfort, or anything else you need. Only as you allow doubt to govern is there lack in your world, for the "Presence" is the Treasure House of your world. It is, and I know it now! From the Ascended State I can see how the "Presence" was acting then, but I did not know it. It enabled Me to have the time for free search. Today I see why that long search was necessary for Me, because it was building up the strength, power, and momentum which I needed when I met this Good Brother.

Your activity in the Acknowledgment of your "Presence" is calling It forth for the accomplishment, as you think, of your problems today. Oh, Dear Hearts, it is beautiful and wonderful; but the accomplishment of solving the problems, do you not see, is only a fragmentary part of it. It is the momentum that you are gaining which is the Victory of the accomplishment of your so-called problems. One day it will stand there in full power and strength for your Final Victory.

Oh, Beloved Ones, do you not see how all is within the great power of the final accumulation of the Energy which enables you to sweep forward into the Freedom of your Victory and Ascension? It is the Victory, the end of all human pilgrimage; for you never again re-embody as you are today, after your Ascension. You have your Eternal Light Body then. You may go where you will in the Universe; and do you not think I have had a good time since?

Beloved Ones, I have not been idle a moment. All of the wonderful Places I have seen in those Great Octaves of Light—the Heaven of Earth! Dear Ones, I have seen such things as are inconceivable to the human mind today. Yet every one of those magnificent things is as tangible and real in those Octaves of Light as your physical places are today.

I bear witness before the World and the Universe!

Even in so short a time I have seen so much; for I have never stopped in the great Acceptance and Glorifying of My World with the actual Knowledge of going from place to place and seeing firsthand all of these great, these marvelous things which the whole World is one day to know. Then, you can understand how great is My Joy for being given this Privilege tonight to speak My Heart to you and to try to have you feel Its Earnestness, Its Joy, Its Happiness, and Gratitude to the Great "Presence," to Saint Germain, and to this Good Brother.

In this great stillness, just let yourselves be flooded by the Glory of My Feeling and Conviction. Accept It, if you will! Qualify It to expand with great earnestness and speed to assist you, to glorify you with all the Courage and Strength which I have and feel in the gaining of My Victory, that It may give you all the Assistance you require for the same great joyous Achievement! Feel the fullness of It sweep into and abide in your being, acting there with full Power and holding you first in Its Great Calmness, and then in Its Joyous Assurance of your Victory; for only in the calmness of your feeling world can you gain quickly the Victory of your "Presence." *Feel It!*

Oh, Great Host of Ascended Masters! Charge My Feeling into the feeling world of these Beloved Ones, all the Students in Los Angeles and southern California. Charge My Feeling into their feeling world — My

Feeling of the Glory and Victory, oh, so recently achieved. Glorify every blessed one who has turned aside from this Light through some falsehood which has been spread to them—bring them back, oh, "Mighty I AM Presence," into this Great Pathway of Light again!

Hold them so firm in Your Consciousness, so firm against the falsehoods that the sinister thing tries to feed into their worlds. Oh, sweep it out, Glorious "Presence" and Great Host of Ascended Masters! Hold these beloved ones and those who have momentarily been drawn aside—hold them in Thy Mighty Tube of Light until no longer can falsehood turn them from the Pathway of Light. Oh, "Mighty I AM Presence," reach out Your Arms and Your Hands; bring into this coming Class [Pan Pacific] these beloved ones who have turned temporarily aside! Glorify them with the Truth which they know in their Hearts, but which through the foolish human intellect accepting falsehood has made them turn aside. Bring them into Thy Great Flood of Light, oh, "Mighty I AM Presence," and give them the strength and courage to stand against the falsehoods which have been uttered! Make them stand forth in their own Freedom and Light.

We make this Call tonight. There shall not anything turn the Students aside from this Great Pathway of Light ever again! So shall I, with the Great Rays of Light, watch over and pour forth such a Power that It will silence forever every discordant thing, every individual, who tries to pour out falsehood concerning these Messengers and the Light. They shall cease, until one day they see their great mistake and turn again to the Light.

Stop the treachery of anyone who would come into the Class of these Loved Ones and then go out and spread falsehood concerning it! That thing shall cease, for I shall watch and stand guard! No longer shall such a thing go on. I love this Good Brother as few can understand in the outer world. I told him I would render the greatest possible Service to him. So shall I, by standing guard to protect him, his loved ones, and the Light which Saint Germain has brought forth. I do it of My own conscious Volition, of My own Great Love and Power, and I am not limited in the Power I shall use! Spread this everywhere, Beloved Ones! Tell the people that David Lloyd, who made His Ascension on Mount Shasta, is standing guard over these Loved Ones and this Light! Let those deal with Me who want to harm them.

I have asked this Good Brother not to repeat My Name, but tonight I give it to you Myself. So, Beloved Ones, stand in the Glory of the Wondrous Light of your "Mighty I AM Presence." Be the fulfilling of the Perfection which It is! You have the strength! You have the Power! Yours is the Joy! Your "Mighty I AM

Presence" will release all the Strength, Courage, and Power you require for any given purpose, if you will but call It forth into action.

Never allow your human to cause you to feel that you cannot draw forth enough Power from your "Presence" to do what you require in your world. It is not true. Your Call does release all the Power you need for any given achievement and for the Glory of your Ascension. Do not let your human qualification act to prevent your entering quickly into full Freedom. "The Light of God never fails," and that Light is your Life!

Today I call forth the fullness of this Great Power. I call forth the Fullness of your "Mighty I AM Presence," to take command of your minds, bodies, your homes, and your worlds; to produce Its Perfection and hold Its Dominion there; to make you dauntless before the face of man, and enable you to refuse acceptance of any discord or falsehood which may be uttered in the world about you!

Stand forth in that Mighty Light and move forth Victorious in the Light, glorifying your home and families with the Glory of the "Presence" which never fails. It could not and never will fail. May Its Light blaze forth from your Heart, filling the world, your world, until there is no longer anything but the Light — "the Light of God that never fails"; the Light that is the "Mighty I AM Presence"; the Light that beats your Heart and is in every cell of your body! EX-PAND, O LIGHT! O LIGHT! O LIGHT! Expand within these loved ones, and assert the Glorification of Thyself, forever sustained. We thank Thee.

THE OLD MAN OF THE
HILLS' DISCOURSE

SINDELARS' GROUP — LOS ANGELES, CALIFORNIA

MARCH 25, 1937

MY CHILDREN, from out the seeming Mysteries of Infinity has come Freedom to mankind, in the Glory of this simplified Instruction which your Beloved Master Saint Germain has brought forth. In all My world of experience, none so great has ever come forth. Think, My Precious Children, today in a World so greatly in need, all symbology and expressions which have been so confusing to mankind have been withheld and will no longer be allowed to act in the World.

That which was once understood through great symbols — and it was once necessary to use them in former cycles — has passed! Mankind today must have the Law of Life in the simplicity of the "Mighty I AM Presence." Oh, Beloved Ones, while I speak to you tonight, will you feel as never before the Mighty Import of those Words — "I AM." The Great, the Greatest Creative Word in the Universe is given into your use without limit. It only remains for you to apply It with firm determination to enable you to stand in the Octave of Light where We do.

226

Think how long We have endeavored to minister to mankind, and yet have seen so little evidence of accomplishment. Even that which has been accomplished was but temporary. Now today, in this Great Knowledge, this Great Wisdom in Its great simplicity which the Beloved Saint Germain has brought forth, mankind shall again be free. Not for more than two hundred thousand years has mankind had such an opportunity! I plead with you, oh, My Children, feel how important it is that you apply, apply, and never weary of applying this Teaching of Saint Germain, which is absolutely certain, and without question will bring you Freedom from every limitation, and then your Ascension.

The struggle of mankind through the past few hundred years has grown more and more fierce, as the vibratory action and speed of all activity has intensified. You yourselves must see and know how great has been that speed. In your language, that "stepped-up" activity has meant so much in transportation. Then, will you realize that within your human forms there has been taking place the same identical activity, in the increased speed of the vibratory action within yourselves? It is the same as has taken place, only in a cruder manner, in your world of transportation.

From the man with the rod and pack upon his back, have come your marvelous airplanes today.

Still more wonderful ones will come forth ere long. Think in how short a period such transcendent progress has been accomplished.

You stand today, Beloved Children of the Light, in the Open Door of so much greater Transcendent Activity. Even that which is within your own scope of comprehension seems small indeed compared to it. You must realize now that in all of the Magnificent Assistance which is being given you, no one should ever for a moment feel discouraged. After having battled the forces that sometimes rock a Planet, then today, when you have before you your freedom, how can anyone ever again feel weary or discouraged?

Do you not understand, oh, Beloved Ones, that through the centuries you have continued to battle these forces of human creation continually? Now you have before you the Remedy—the certain, definite, sure Remedy. How can you hesitate? How can you ever feel—ever again—doubt or fear? With the Knowledge of the Greatest "Presence" in the Universe which gives you Life and beats your Heart, how can you ever again fear?

I, tonight, give forth to the Beloved Students of California, America, and the World, in My Humble Way, My Assistance to enable you to be free, more determined in your Application, and yet always with a great calm serenity which knows the Mastery of conditions which have heretofore terrified you. Such is your right, such is your privilege, such is your authority, your ability. Will you allow Me, tonight, to give you such Strength that no one in California who is earnest in his Application of the Light will ever feel again one moment's doubt or fear? It seems strange how sometimes lovely Students of the Light will accept human suggestions that make them doubt this Great Truth which Saint Germain has brought forth. They even doubt the great honest sincerity of this Good Brother, who has brought forth the Great Reality of the Law to mankind in being the observer of the Great Law of Life.

Last night, those who were present had such a transcendent privilege of hearing One who has so recently achieved the Ascension, describe to you Her Experience. Beloved Ones, no longer waver, but with firmness and unyielding determination go forward in the Radiance of your own "Mighty I AM Presence." There is naught that can stop you! Nothing can interfere with you or prevent you having your quick and sure freedom! Oh, I plead with you, do not longer listen to human gossip and suggestions which make you waver and feel disturbed. The pity! Oh, the pity that mankind will longer gossip or accept vicious suggestions of another.

We are striving so earnestly to help you to set yourselves free, but without your cooperation and obedience it cannot be done. Your Free Will must be utilized—and joyously—in order for you, oh, Precious Ones, to reach the Glory of Eternal Light and Freedom. We, who have watched through the centuries, century after century pouring forth, sometimes feel great Joy at the accomplishment. Then again, We see mankind relapse into the chains of their own creation.

This time the Light's Victory is permanent, and do you realize all of this is due to your Beloved Saint Germain? No one else chose to go forth and take the consequences of success or failure! He did! He won the battle! Praises ever be to Him! Why was it so? Because under the Great Cosmic Law, being of the Seventh Ray, He was the One to try it out. When He said to the Beloved Messengers: "I have started this Great Law in Action; My Success now depends upon you, whether you are strong enough to stand with Me"—and they have been.

As the Beloved Messenger reminded you tonight, you have now become the Guardians of this Light. We shall be happy to give you the Assistance to be the full Guardians of the Light which has done such wonderful work in California.

Now I must, because it is the Law, commend Mrs. Fisher in New York and Mrs. Ekey in Philadelphia for the transcendent work that they have recently accomplished, because it has made it possible for the Messengers to go there again. How wonderful it is to know how the Great Law raises up those who are strong enough to go forth dauntless before human creation, which deprives so many of their Freedom in the Light.

Today, you beloved ones in California have banded together in these very wonderful Groups of people. The Light, when you are gathered as you are in this room tonight, from the Higher Octaves becomes a dazzling, blazing Sun of Light. Would you believe that, and would you like to see It? One day you shall!

The human is so strange, is it not? It so hesitates to accept what it cannot feel and handle. Yet the greatest thing in the world in all activity is that which is invisible! You all know this! The Life that gives you activity, you do not see It, do you? The radio which carried the lovely Message tonight from the lovely Messenger — you did not see its activity, but you heard it! Then do you not see how in all of the greatest activities, all Life's action is invisible? Yet you have the use, blessing, and benefit of it.

Look at your great motors, look at your great engines. You do not see the operations going on in them — I mean the one who is not familiar with them, not the engineer; yet those who ride upon the train or within the airplanes, you are not as a rule familiar with that activity which is going on in the engine as it carries you through the air or over the rails to your destination. Yet you accept it and use its blessing.

Let us be very practical tonight, that once and forever there may be erased from your consciousness, whatever causes doubts and fears within you. Why do human beings continue to let the accumulated suggestion of mankind dominate them—for that alone causes fear and doubt? Do you think the Life which beats your Heart accepts doubt or fear? It cannot. Then what is it? Just the accumulation of human consciousness.

Now today you understand how to enfold yourselves in Light's Invincible Protection, and how to use the Violet Consuming Flame to free yourselves from all discordant accumulation. If you will not do it, then you must remain in your limitations; but I plead with you—you who have been so earnest—use this! Do not cease when you are so near your Wondrous Victory.

Remember, your world is a world of your own. You are calling forth the Action of your "Presence." Thus you can and are surely clearing your world of all accumulation of the centuries. I plead with you, continue until the fullness of your achievement is attained. Then you will feel the great Outpouring from your "Presence" acting more and more quickly, until no longer does any doubt or fear touch your consciousness.

This Good Brother is a living proof before you, and those who knew him years ago know the Victory

that is his. You can all do it. We have watched him
pleading, pleading, pleading with the people to stand
guard over their worlds, to shut out all inharmony,
that the full, Pure, Perfect Energy and Substance of
the "Presence" can flow forth to fill their worlds with
the Perfection which the "Presence" is. He will continue until you realize the Glory of the Scepter of the
"Mighty I AM Presence" is in your hands, to command your world to be free.

Beloved Ones, tarry no longer! Arise in the Glory
and the Light of your "Mighty I AM Presence"! Apply this Law with determination, and never can Victory be withheld from you. Do you not see, Beloved
Ones, it is only as you waver, that disturbance in-
trudes? Out of the Glory which is yours, oh, Beloved
Ones, comes all that is good! Never doubt for a second that every Assistance through the power of Radiation is being poured forth to you constantly, and
no sincere effort is ever lost. Every step you are gaining is sustained. You cannot slip back!

Tonight, in the great calm atmosphere by which
you are surrounded, in the great stillness and quiet
which all need so much, you who have had difficulty
in stilling your outer self will find much less difficulty
in the future from tonight, with this Contact. May
I remind you just why these many Dictations have
come forth in such rapid succession? To charge you
and your world! For while you are listening to the

various Ones, a great Consuming Activity is going on. How and why? Because you have made the Call for the Violet Consuming Flame to dissolve and consume all discord and undesirable things from your world. So now in this Call can the Assistance be given.

It is a joyous thing to see what is taking place as the various Ones have dictated to you, each One supplying a certain Quality that you need. Think of it, that you may feel—I know most of you do—that all may feel the deepest gratitude possible. Dear Ones, think what it means for all these Great Beings to take the time from Their Great Cosmic Activities to come forth and give you the Assistance which They do in these activities. Think of it! Think what it means to you! As you feel the greater and greater gratitude, praise, and thanks, you will feel how much easier it is for you to make your Application; to feel the courage and confidence you require; to give more dynamic feeling, and therefore produce more rapid results.

You cannot fail ever in your Application! We, from the Ascended State, are also decreeing this for you. Look! As you are decreeing for yourselves and for mankind, then do you not see, Precious Ones, that you have opened your Door for Us to not only pour forth through the Light Rays the Radiance to you, but you have made the way definite for Us to give you the Assistance which your Hearts so greatly crave?

Now because We do not immediately pick you up and set you into Eternal Freedom and Opulence, do not think that the work is not going on just the same. If We did that, you would cease making conscious effort, would you not? Until the human is fully dissolved, it will assert itself if the human form is given nothing to do. That is why the Messengers and We are calling forth action into your Life and world, because you must be active in something, Dear Hearts. Your mind must be occupied in some constructive activity if you want to have the greatest results.

Sometimes individuals make the great mistake of endeavoring to call forth the "Presence" all the hours of the day. That is not wise. You do not have to keep calling the "Presence" all day long, except where you are giving your twenty-four hour service. That of course is a very marvelous thing; but I mean in individuals' own lives. Do you not see, Precious Ones, how if you will utilize morning, noon, and night to give forth your dynamic Decrees and Application for that which you require, then give your attention to the other activities of the day, you will find wonderful, wonderful results? Sometimes individuals in their great earnestness keep in meditation too long; or they keep revolving things in their thought and feeling until unknowingly, they make the things they do not want more real than the things they do.

Be so practical, Beloved Ones, in all that you do.

When you apply, apply dynamically, firmly; then go on with your other outer activities, until you feel impelled again. Then give it again. With firm determination call your "Presence" to take command of you and give you today the perfect thing every hour of the day. You will soon come into the marvelous Application which will not weary you, but will keep you in great joyous contentment continually. That is what We so much desire you to do.

Now watch, will you, every one of you? If you begin to feel weary in your Acknowledgment of the "Presence," it is because the human is trying to be the doer. If you become discouraged, it is the human. Then simply say: " 'Mighty I AM Presence,' now You are the Doer, through my attention to Thee. All things are in Your Hands. You take command and see that the perfect thing is done, and that I do the perfect things also." Then you will have no difficulty, I assure you.

Remember! We who have come forth to speak Our Wishes to you, have made Ourselves a part of you. Think of it! We have willingly made Ourselves a part of you. Now you will not disappoint Us, will you? You would not think of disappointing Us in this Perfection which We decree for you. Therefore, will you buckle on your armor, the Strength of your "Mighty I AM Presence," Its Courage, Its Dominion, and let It act to your great Joy and Freedom forever?

In the fullness of the Great Light which is the Light within every cell of your body, I command It to take on definite action for your Freedom; to expand in Divine Order until all the density with which you have clothed yourself, clothed the Light—the Light pattern of your human form—is dissolved and you stand forth Free in the Radiance of your "Presence"!

Will you not accept this tonight as I call It forth for you, to become Eternally Sustained and Active for your blessing, happiness, and freedom? Feel the full Glory of It acting within you this instant, and glorify It with Me, to be Eternally Sustained and Active there, to produce Its perfect results without limit—that all human accumulations about you be now dissolved; that you go forth a Free Being of Light, which you are; and in the Mighty Directing Intelligence of your "Mighty I AM Presence," receive, be, and act Its Mighty Glory.

When you wish to determine your activity, say, "Would the Ascended Masters do this?"—and you will have no difficulty in determining your field and mode of action. Be free from all human limitations this night! Accept the Full Freedom which is yours, and do not, I plead with you, allow any activity to take place in your feeling world that will in any wise annul this which is offered! Accept, feel, and be the Free Glory of your "Mighty I AM Presence" which is released to you this night.

I charge this activity of the *Voice of the "I AM"* with the Mighty Perfection of the "Mighty I AM Presence," the Ascended Host of Masters, the Legion of Light, and the Cosmic Beings—that this remain in a mighty harmonious activity, that no human creation has any power to qualify it with anything but Harmony and Perfection, that the feeling of its activity and blessing to mankind may ever expand, until all mankind know the *Voice of the "I AM"!*

Your Beloved Master Jesus decreed that this Magazine go forth. Your Beloved Brother Mr. Sindelar accepted the responsibility and the charge. Then you, as Students of the Light, it is for you to pour forth such a blessing that only harmony reigns within the midst of his activity in the tremendous work which is required. Will you not join with Me in this always, and see that no quality of criticism ever goes forth against him or against Mrs. Ballard, who works so ceaselessly and earnestly so this material may go forth in a beautiful, marvelous manner for your blessing and that of mankind?

Remember, Beloved Ones, these blessed ones work night and day so these things may go forth on time. Yet there are those so unfortunate as to criticize them if a few days have passed beyond the time expected. Remember, Beloved Children, My Children, you are Guardians of this Light! You are Guardians of the

Voice of the "I AM" as It goes forth to bless all mankind. Then if you allow discord or criticism to pass your lips, you have joined the sinister activity to longer withhold the Glory which the Great Radiance poured forth through the *Voice of the "I AM"* brings.

Beloved Ones, My Gratitude is boundless for those who have been willing to send forth the Books without limit everywhere. Remember, Loved Ones, every Magazine has a definite, powerful Activity in It to bless mankind. It is sent forth with that purpose, with that intent. Each one has a glorious Activity within Itself. So, Beloved Ones, spread this everywhere; and when one would feel impatient, silence it by reminding them of the nights and days these blessed ones serving work, that these things may be accomplished.

Now that your Decree Book will soon be out, oh, Beloved Ones, APPLY! APPLY! APPLY them, until nothing in the world stands before you or between you and your "Presence"! Only as you apply, Beloved Ones, can you have your freedom. No one else can do it for you. Everyone can help, but you alone are the decreer of what shall be in your world. Feel it definitely. Give your Command! Stand by it until the fullness of that Decree finds manifestation in you and your world! Stand glorified forever in the fullness of the Mighty Power which is your "Mighty I AM Presence." There is no other Power in the Universe to act but that—your

"Mighty I AM Presence."

So remind the outer often that no longer can it have even a suggestion which would disturb you in your onward Application and freedom. It is rushing unto you and your world through your Acknowledgment of the "Presence." As you continue to hold harmony in your feelings, nothing can stop the Glory of your "Presence" rushing forward like a mighty avalanche into your world to produce Its Perfection, hold Its Dominion, and supply you with every good thing in the World.

I ask you tonight, oh, Beloved Ones, even more intensely than you have been calling, call the "Mighty I AM Presence" to reach out Its Hands everywhere and bring subscribers to the *Voice of the "I AM,"* that all mankind may be blessed! Do you not realize, oh, My Precious Ones, that in your Call for the "Mighty I AM Presence" to reach Its Hands out everywhere and bring in subscribers to this Magazine, the Mightiest Power in the Universe is set into action to produce it?

Again with your supply of money or whatever is required, Precious Ones, call your "Mighty I AM Presence" to release limitless abundance from Its Treasure House—to reach out and bring into your use the supply you require, through the Power of Divine Love. You cannot be deprived of that which you require for your use and happiness. It is a great Law of your Life, oh, Beloved Ones. It is not anyone's opinion, but a

Great Law of your Life that must be, must act at your Call, must answer your Decree, must fulfill your requirements when called into action with earnest determination. It shall be done!

In the fullness of the Blessings of Infinite Light, I enfold you, all Students in California, America, and the World! I send forth to New York and Philadelphia the Glory of the Radiance which I wield, to bless, to expand those mighty activities there, until all may be saved from that which is threatening.

Great Infinite Cosmic Light! Come forth before these blessed Students of the "I AM"! Clear the way! Set them firmly upon their Pathway of Light! Hold them there dauntless until their full power of achievement is attained. We thank Thee it is done and sustained forever, unto the Perfection and Ascension of everyone. We thank Thee.

OUR BELOVED BOB'S
DISCOURSE

YOUNG PEOPLE'S 100% GROUP — GLENDALE, CALIFORNIA
MARCH 26, 1937

MY BELOVED Brothers and Sisters in the Light, tonight is My night of Joy in being able to convey to you something of that which I have experienced since this Beloved Messenger came to the Rayborn home. In My contact with him and then with Saint Germain, how little the first day when he came into Mr. Rayborn's mine, did I realize what was to follow. You beloved ones today cannot possibly imagine in your outer human sense the Beauty, the Perfection, and the Successful Achievement which is before you in your Acknowledgment and Application of the Law of your "Mighty I AM Presence."

I shall never forget the first touch of this Knowledge of which I became outwardly aware. It was when this Good Brother came to the mine with Mr. Rayborn and selected the spot where the tunnel was to be driven in—where I thought it was not possible for any value to be. Yet afterwards it proved the Wisdom of Saint Germain, even to the exact number of feet the tunnel was to be driven to reach the ore body. The tunnel did reach it and every particle of it was exactly as He said it would be.

Can you imagine what it meant to Me when I saw it all fulfilled? I am frank to say I thought Mr. Rayborn was crazy when he started that tunnel, because from a geological standpoint it was thought to be impossible for such a thing to occur. Yet it was, and is there today.

Now to return to Our Work: At the time We left for Arabia and India, We met the Beloved Leto our first night out on the Atlantic, at dinner. She immediately took us into training and taught us how to leave the body consciously and at will—and what rejoicing We experienced! I presume I was the most enthusiastic of all, for when I found I could get out of that body and be free, I did not lose any more time. It is such a joyful thing, Beloved Ones, to know that you—the Real You—are not bound to your physical body when you understand the Law and how to operate It.

Our Beloved Lady Master Leto with such great Grace and Kindliness taught Us the very first evening how to do it. We were able to go and come from the body from that time on, without further Assistance. Your Higher Mental Body, Dear Ones, is the Thinker, the Doer of all that is good. While your physical bodies might have all the faculties still in them, yet without that Stream of Energy governed by your Higher Mental Body, your "Presence," you would not be able to move your hand or anything else.

This is one thing I wish to convey to you tonight: Everything depends upon the Acknowledgment of your "Presence"; for then your Higher Mental Body has the full Power and Authority to release whatever Mighty Intelligent Energy you require into your outer world and activity. Without such Acknowledgment, only enough energy goes forth to just sustain Life. Do you not see, Beloved Ones, how ordinary people without this Understanding of the "Presence" are using less than ten percent of the great Energy which is ready for their use? Is it not too ridiculous, too stupid for words, to think that we have not reached out with enough intensity even to God—all Light— to release these Great Inner Powers which all of us have?

With Myself, when the awakening started, it was so tremendous—and I, without knowing it, was so ready—that after the first experience of which I just spoke, concerning the activity of Mr. Rayborn, it seemed to Me there never was another doubt in My whole feeling world. I accepted everything else from then on readily and joyfully. Of course that accounts for My rapid progress and the Expansion of My own Light which took place.

Then we arrived in Arabia, in that wonderful place. Just try for a moment to feel this as I give you a little general description of how I actually felt, for I still retain that marvelous feeling. When we were driving along over the desert — nothing in sight anywhere but the low hills some distance away — suddenly the floor of the desert opened like the jaws of a great creature, and our automobile drove right in; the great jaw closed, and the desert floor was as usual.

Dear Hearts, can you imagine the feeling of one knowing so little about this Great Law as I did, when I suddenly began experiencing the marvels which came through It? Then We went into that great buried city and the great rooms underneath. There everything was spotless, and the Great Ones were moving about doing Their Work.

In Retreats of that kind, those who are serving rarely speak a word unless spoken to, because they have learned the Law of Silence and the waste of Energy which goes on through the general chatter of mankind, for it is of no particular consequence. When We observed them working, I realized as never before what a Great Being Saint Germain was.

I had seen Him do many wonderful things. The dinner He precipitated at the mine in Mr. Rayborn's little bungalow was a marvelous thing; but the things that followed afterwards were so much more wonderful. Today what seemed so wonderful at first is quite commonplace now. They do such marvelous things in teaching the Students the use of the Light

Rays. They can project Them, for They are tangible Substance, Dear Hearts! Remember always in your use of the Light, that Divine Love and Light — which are synonymous — are Self-luminous, Intelligent Substance. Therefore, when you pour out a great volume of Divine Love to someone you love — a person, place, condition, or thing — the Self-luminous, Intelligent Substance enfolds that one in the Perfection which It is. It produces for you and for them a wondrous activity.

You have all heard the Promptings of the Ascended Masters to use Their Ascended Master Consciousness. You must no doubt realize that this means the identical Self-luminous, Intelligent Substance of which We are speaking. The Consciousness of the Ascended Masters is the Substance which is charged with the Consciousness of Their Victory through Self-conscious attainment — Their Ascension.

Now mark you, when you call the Ascended Masters' Consciousness and Substance into action in your mind, body, and your world, that carries with It the Consciousness of Their Achievement. Therefore, do you not see, Beloved Ones, that in calling forth the Ascended Masters' Consciousness to your assistance, you are charging yourself and world with that consciousness which has already attained? Then, you see, it is so much easier and you will more readily turn and use these simple Laws of your "Mighty

I AM Presence" for the Expansion of your own Light.

In the use of the Light Rays, it so happened that We all chose to render the same Service, which the Divine Director Himself said was unusual. Therefore, in Our Service since, it has been almost indescribable, the things which We have been able to accomplish individually, in state and government. This has all been done through the projection of Light Rays, which, mark you again—do not ever forget this—are Self-luminous, Intelligent Substance.

If I were to tell you some of the things that had been done in the recent strikes, and show you how the Substance of these Light Rays dissolves discord and enables individuals to reach an adjustment, you would be not only greatly delighted, but rejoice at this Service which is being rendered. It is steadily and surely dissolving and dispelling all of the vicious, discordant qualities generated by mankind. Those qualities are being used today by that which you know as the sinister force to still try to drive its destruction into mankind.

Therefore, Precious Ones, you do have sufficient understanding to call forth, as you see in the Chart, those Rays of Light pouring out from the "Presence." You can now begin to call forth those Light Rays from the "Presence," for They are Self-luminous, Intelligent Substance. When you call the "Presence" into action to project Them to a given point, you are rendering the identical Service that We render, only in a lesser degree. The "Presence" will always perform whatever Service you require.

Do not let your human self cause you to doubt or question, when you have called these Light Rays forth; for It will do all you require and quickly. As you practice this, you will find that you have at your finger tips the use of a Great Law. It will delight you and give you the greatest possible Happiness and Freedom—far greater than anything the outer world has to offer today!

The happiness of the human senses is but fragmentary, Beloved Ones. So few years ago, I Myself knew nothing in the outer consciousness about these Great Laws. Yet today I am able to apply Them with such astonishing Results that I never cease to marvel at it Myself. Because of the previous preparation and Expansion of My own Light, it was possible for Me to enter quickly into this Activity with Rex, My sister, and Nada.

The joke on Me was that Pearl, My sister, was being trained years before I ever dreamed of it. Even from a little girl, Saint Germain was training her. Yet she kept it perfectly silent from every living soul on Earth. When she came to Me at the mine, then We discovered she had known Saint Germain for many years already.

So Dear Ones, in mentioning these personal

experiences to you, I want you to realize how little the outer self knows what is actually going on about it. Once your attention is called to this "Mighty I AM Presence" which beats your Heart, anything in the world, Beloved Ones, might take place for you. No one in the outer knows your preparation or how great the Light has expanded within you.

Tonight it has been My Privilege to observe your Light; and that is why We can, from this night, be of much greater Service to you. We see the expansion of the Light within each one of you, and know what is necessary to be done to give you the greatest Assistance. Will you not feel how much We love you, and how much We want to render you any Service which is possible and the Law of your being permits, that you too may quickly enter into the Freedom which We now experience?

Oh, Dear Ones, I wish the Law of your being permitted Me to say certain things to you tonight which I observe here. Your joy would be boundless; but you must make your Application, for only by that do you gain the permanent Victory. This is the same reason why Saint Germain would not do certain things for these Beloved Messengers. Because in the necessity of the outer world, you are compelled to make the Application which you would not do otherwise, if you had all within your use that you desired. Therefore, in your Application the Energy is released which builds a momentum that makes for your final Victory and the Ascension.

Just as the Good Brother [David Lloyd] who spoke the other night explained to you, that through His long search He gained the momentum that enabled Him to attain the Final Victory—today, in your Application and through your attention held on your "Mighty I AM Presence," you are building a momentum which makes for your marvelous, wonderful Victory. You will achieve It! You would be amazed, some of you precious ones, if you knew the Service you could render. You know one gets sorely tempted sometimes to tell you; but only as the Law of your being permits, is it done. Tonight will you accept from Me the Encouragement, Strength, and Assurance which I know must be for your definite, certain Victory?

As you go forward in your Application of the Great Law, there are a few things which are essential. Refuse absolutely, as I see so many of you are doing, to listen to any gossip or discordant voicing of anything that comes to your ears! Refuse acceptance of it into your world! Refuse to send out discordant feeling to anything, any condition, or anyone! Then you keep yourself so harmonized, that as you call your "Presence" forth into action, Its Powers flow through like a rushing river.

You know, when you lift a gate in a dam, the water

rushes forth. Your harmonious feeling maintained and your Call to the "Presence" are just like lifting the floodgates of your being; for the Mighty Power of the "Presence" rushes forth into your world, giving the Service you require. Your Call to your "Presence" is just as definite! Because you do not see It, makes no difference. The "Presence" acts and the Energy acts! Hereafter, in your Call to the "Mighty I AM Presence," will you not feel this? Feel, every time you call to your "Presence," that you simply lift the floodgates of your being and Its great Inner Power rushes forth to release the Service you require. I Myself have had tremendous results from this feeling, and if it will help you, then I shall be glad.

Anyone who has ever had his attention called to the "Mighty I AM Presence" can no longer be in limitation of any kind. He need not experience any kind of ill health. The instant some appearance of distress comes within yourself, or an appearance of limitation enters into your outer world, refuse acceptance of it; give it no energy to act in your world. Say to any disturbance in your body, "Get out! I refuse acceptance of all disturbance!" And it will obey positively.

As you practice this, you will have no difficulty in controlling not only the feelings in your body, but the energy which goes out into your world. You will learn to feel such a definite focus from here—your

Heart Center—that It will be like a Ray of Light going out and holding Its Focus of Light steady until the work is accomplished. It is the easiest, most wonderful way of accomplishment, Beloved Ones, that could ever be conceived for mankind.

You no longer have to struggle and battle with the things of the outer world when you call the "Presence" into action to hold you firm in the Pathway of Light. Clear out of your Pathway of Light everything discordant. Call your "Presence" to take you forward quickly into all you wish to achieve, and you will have no difficulty in doing it. Your "Presence" knows no resistance or interference, and when you call It into action, It goes forth anywhere in the Universe to fulfill your Call.

If you are not having results, remember in your feeling world there is something obstructing the way. Then call the "Presence" to take out of your world whatever the obstruction is. Then, the Power of the "Presence" will flow on to do Its Perfect Work. You are not subject, Precious Ones, any longer to the conditions which exist in the outer world!

You beloved ones who are musical or have artistic talents, utilize this Knowledge of the "Presence" to Its fullest extent! Everyone can speak and sing with the Voice of the "Mighty I AM Presence." For your hands, if you are artistically inclined or wish to play instrumental music, say: " 'Mighty I AM Presence,' these are Your Hands! Take command of them! Produce Your Perfect Harmonies, Your Perfect Beauty and Perfection through them." Then you will make your hands a perfect channel for your "Mighty I AM Presence" to use, and the most wonderful things in the world will be produced.

In My experience up until I met Saint Germain, I had not the slightest inclination to paint, and apparently no artistic temperament; but recently, I produced one of the most remarkable paintings, which I hope one day to bring forth into visibility for you. I found that whatever I called for, comes forth into action. This is what I want you to feel. Anything upon which your attention is fixed, the "Presence" will bring forth and produce the results—whether it be in music, art, the supply you require, or whatever the activity is.

It matters not, for the "Presence" will produce the result for you through the power of your attention, your vision, and qualification; but do not allow your human self at any time to interfere with that. When you make your Decree, stand by it! When you call your "Presence" into action to perform a certain service, stand by it; for nothing can stop it but yourself!

Tonight, Precious Ones, may I convey to you the Love from Pearl, Nada, Rex, Mr. and Mrs. Rayborn, and David Lloyd, who love you so greatly. They will be of great Assistance to you and all the young people of America. One day all the "I AM" Students, all young people will meet in one great conclave! Maybe you think I am prophesying—I am not prophesying; but it will be! It will be a very wonderful thing! You know, when the Ascended Masters plan something, it always works out. Is not that a wonderful thing to know? There is no human obstruction that can get in Their way. So We want you to feel this, if you will.

Remember, Beloved Ones, the Law of Life is Harmony. Harmony maintained is the Infinite Invitation for the Glory of your "Presence" to flood forth into your world, produce Its Perfection, and hold Its Dominion forever. Nothing in the world can interfere with it but yourself! The only way you can interfere with it is by inharmony in your feeling. That is easy enough for your "Presence" to control, if you will call It into action to do it.

Precious Ones, in the removing of habits or anything that you wish to get rid of, your "Presence" is the Power that does it. You but call the "Presence" into action to take out of you the desire which caused the habit, and to replace it by the Perfection of the "Presence." No matter what it is that has been accumulated in your Life, you do not care, because the "Presence" will take out the desire and replace it by the Ascended Masters' Satisfaction and Perfection.

This is how you can have everything that is beautiful, happy, and perfect in your Life, expressed and acting there every moment. If you so choose you can do it, and it is sure. Call your "Presence" into action to produce the results, because the human of itself does not have the sustaining power to maintain Perfection. *Whatever the human does is but temporary; but by calling your "Presence" into action, you can have a sustained activity.*

It is because of the temporary action of the human that mankind has had relief and then the illness or condition returns. This has occurred simply because individuals did not know the Sustaining Power or Qualification. Before they knew it, the feelings became discordant and they began to accept the old condition again in the feeling. Then the whole thing recoiled. This is not so in your Understanding of the "Presence," when calling It into Action.

So tonight, with all the Love of My Heart, I convey to you the Love and Blessings of those who love you so much more than you can know in the outer, and who stand ready to give every Assistance. When you have called the "Mighty I AM Presence" into action, do not hesitate to call upon any of Us; and whatever Assistance We can give, you may be sure will be given.

We want you to go forth so victorious, so marvelous in your achievement! Do not let the human opinions of the outer world govern you. Stand firm in your "Mighty I AM Presence," calling It forth into action;

and do not allow anyone to make you feel that you are being deprived of any human sense activity. That is where you need to be firm and stand your ground against the suggestion of people who do not understand this Law. Such great strength is within you that I am sure no one of you will have any difficulty in holding your own in and with your "Mighty I AM Presence." With all the Love of Our Beings, We pour forth to you like a Mighty River Its Eternal Perfection. I thank you.

SAINT GERMAIN'S DISCOURSE

PAN PACIFIC CLASS — LOS ANGELES, CALIFORNIA

APRIL 4, 1937

BELOVED Students of Los Angeles, great is My Privilege this day in voicing to you My Gratitude, My Boundless Gratitude for your sincerity, your loyalty to the Light, to your own "Mighty I AM Presence," and to My Humble Efforts. A great fruition is taking place, after so many centuries of effort. Not until this Understanding of the "Mighty I AM Presence" had been brought forth could mankind be sustained, or even that which was temporarily accomplished, be made permanent.

So, I give you these Words today as an eternal—an everlasting—stabilizing, encouraging Power to act within you and your world and produce the Perfection which you, through your Heart, desire. It is a long, long time since there has been released through the human forms of mankind such a Loyalty and Radiance as has come forth in this Class. I want you to know that for your own encouragement. When I see the precious, beloved Students willing to even make sacrifices to give assistance for the broadcasts which will reach so many people, then My Heart thrills with Joy and a Gratitude which shall ever enfold you; and the Powers that I understand and wield shall enfold you!

From this Class there begins a Mighty Activity. We have asked permission of the Great Cosmic Light to encompass you today in the beginning of Its Action tomorrow. Thus shall you feel and have today that which will come into Its fullness of action tomorrow. Never in the history of mankind has there been the willing attention, obedience, and the great sincere interest in the Light that is being shown today. By the return of the Messengers to you in July, you will feel, or will have felt, many wonderful things.

You are beginning to realize, Beloved Ones, that this is not just another activity brought forth; but It is a permanent, established, Mighty Activity which is expanding within you and will always continue to expand. Even those who temporarily turn aside, through listening to foolish gossip, will return again and see their great mistake. So, Dear Ones, stand within your "Presence," untouched by human gossip or interference, knowing that all is within your grasp in the acceptance of your "Presence" and Its Application. The practicing of your "Presence" is the greatest thing on Earth.

Do you realize today what you have done in enabling this broadcast to go forth in New York? I think not, but ere long I am sure you will. You have heard mentioned throughout the many years and centuries, the idea of brotherly Love. Is there anything greater than that? Is there anything greater than the Service you have rendered here? You are willing to make possible the spreading of this Knowledge to enable thousands and perhaps millions to hear It who would never have contacted the Work in perhaps many years otherwise. Aside from the Mighty Decrees which you have been issuing, doing so much for mankind and yourselves, you are transcending even that, in giving this to a still greater number of mankind.

I try to call this to your attention, not for any human praise, but because of the great Reality of the Light within you which has responded to the necessity and the requirement. You shall be blessed, Beloved Ones, you who have been so generous, for I shall see that you are blessed in ways which you do not know.

We from the Ascended Masters' Octave of Life, having accomplished Our Victory here, We must have the cooperation of mankind in order to release the greatest Power which We know and understand how to use. Only through your Call to the "Presence" can We release sufficient Power to govern the conditions that are confronting you today.

So much has been accomplished since the Messengers were in Honolulu that should I suddenly flash before you the achievement, you would remember it forever. I want you to know that this is no idle thing. It is no human concept or someone's imagination, but a Mighty Activity of the Law of Life and Love which has gone into Action.

Your part of it has been tremendous in your willing obedience to call and call and call. Through your Group Decrees, such a volume of Intelligent Energy and Substance has been released into the mental and feeling world of mankind as to perform a Service almost indescribable. May I remind you today that in calling forth through your Decrees this Mighty Activity of the "Presence" and the Ascended Masters, you are charging into the mental and feeling world this Mighty, Self-luminous, Intelligent Ascended Master Substance and that from the Great Love Star.

This means only that substance remains to be purified which you have qualified in the past. Only it has power to longer act within your world. May I repeat those Words: "No longer has any qualification power to act in your world except that which has been accumulated up to this point." This means that former discordant causes cannot have any substance in the future to act in your world, because of your Call for the Substance from the Ascended Masters' Octave of Life.

The Divine Director, who will dictate to you tonight, has rendered a Service unparalleled thus far. It has been done through your love poured out in this

Class and the love from the rest of the sincere "I AM" Students through America and the World.

To Us, you must understand, there is no time nor space. We go to and fro in the World in Our Ascended Master Bodies—just as tangible, however, as yours. We require no time nor space. By that, I mean We may go from one part of the World to the other in two to three or four minutes, and that is what mankind needs to know today. They need to know this Freedom is for them! As you enter more and more into this Great and Mighty Consciousness of your Mighty "Presence," you will come to understand and feel thoroughly that the same Freedom and Dominion is for you.

It is amazing how mankind continues to believe that things to which it has not been accustomed, are impossible—just because they have not previously had information concerning such things, or their attention has not been called to them. You will find that you yourselves, ere many years are over your heads, will do exactly what you think today is impossible for you to accomplish. I am calling your attention to this now that you may watch it, if you will.

Again, I say to you: this is no idle imagination. It is a Mighty Power gone into action—your Power, your "Mighty I AM Presence." We, who have accomplished the Victory, stand ever ready to encourage, to strengthen, to give you of Our Life to sustain and encourage you unto your Victory, and even your Ascension.

Oh, I plead with you, Beloved Students of the Light who have been in this Light for a year or more: never allow your human self or anyone else to cause you to question for one second your ability to make your Ascension, even in this embodiment. I tell you again that age as you know it, has nothing whatever to do with it. The Expansion of the Light within you has everything to do with it, and the human self knows nothing about that.

As the Messenger has so often said to you, do not limit yourself as to what the "Presence" can do for you and through you. Do not longer give power to limiting appearances. You have entered into a Mighty Stream of Light. It is All-powerful; but you still have Free Will. You still have the ability to operate your power of qualification. If you are not willing to give obedience to Harmony and hold It within your feelings, then you but delay the achievement and must wait that much longer.

I want to say a Word or two, a few Words, to you who are in these Groups. The pledges you take are to your "Presence" and no one else. Do not, I plead with you, go into those Groups out of curiosity, unless you are willing to fulfill that requirement to which you have put your name. You do not understand yet what it means, or the Action of the Law, when unfaithful to your own Light. Your Heart has always been willing, but now your intellect has said, "Yes, I am willing to abide by this." Remember, you are acting under the Law of your Great "Presence," the All-Seeing Eye of God, your "Mighty I AM Presence," from which no single motive or act is hidden.

Sometimes the Messengers have pled with the beloved Students so long, yet they will go on doing the things that they know in their Hearts are a tragic mistake. They think that no one knows it. We cannot help knowing what is within your motive, what is within your world — for it is imprinted on the atmosphere about you, because every thought, feeling, and motive is a record which We have to read. Not that We seek to do it, but if We are going to help you, We must read it. Will you not feel now today, and hold it forever, that the All-Seeing Eye of God, which your Higher Mental Body uses, knows every single thing that occurs in your Life, every feeling and motive that is there? Do not try to deceive your "Presence"!

I am speaking with all the Love of My Heart, for I want to help you. I want you to see, if you will, the mistake of just humanly entering into a thing without a pure, honest motive back of it. Remember, in your Heart Center, as well as in the Heart Center of the Staff who serve these two Messengers, must come purity, loyalty, and faithfulness if you are to go forward in the Light! Deception is an unpardonable thing anywhere in the World, and above all in the Students who have come to know their "Mighty I AM Presence."

So if you have made mistakes (this is the point in which I am trying to help), if you have made mistakes — and you know, the Heart always knows — there is no one who can make excuses for it. Self-pity and vanity are out. They have no part in this Work! Therefore I want you to feel that I hold your hand to help you overcome all these things. If you have made mistakes, call immediately on the Law of Forgiveness and ask the "Presence" to wipe them out, dissolve and consume cause and effect of that mistake or any other. We are watching very closely all the Students, and We know every one that is not sincere.

So Precious Ones, let Us help you, will you not? Will you not call on the Law of Forgiveness for any mistakes you have made? Then with your face to the Light, with your attention to the "Presence," call Its Mighty Powers and Intelligence into action to give you Self-control, Discriminating Intelligence, Mastery over your human desires. Then will you go forward quickly into the full Freedom and Glory which is yours.

I am taking this opportunity today to talk to you very close in your Heart. I feel your Heartbeat while I talk to you, for in that I am trying earnestly to help you free yourself in every way possible today. The Great Divine Director has rendered you a Transcendent Service. Only when you have made the Ascension will you see how great it is.

Think of it, oh, My Precious Ones, of all the centuries that mankind has been compelled one by one to go into the Retreats, away from the discord of the outer world in order to gain this Victory. Now this Knowledge of the "I AM" is brought forth. There is also being given the Assistance of the Great Divine Director and the Others who have come forth to assist the Great Cosmic Light in the Perfect Work It must do for mankind. Mankind need not fail if individuals will give attention to the "Presence" as they have been directed.

In setting aside the third year for you, there has been released a Blessing never before given to mankind. You have noticed, at least you have heard Us mention step by step certain accomplishments for you. That again is not any imagination, but a Mighty Reality. Today as I speak to you, My Heart throbs with greatest Joy and Gratitude that you have been able to so bring yourselves into the Requirement that the Divine Director could do this for you. Not only has this Help been given to you here, but also to the "I AM" Students throughout America and the World. How and why? Because of your Mighty Decrees going forth in the mental and feeling world of mankind and being issued uniform throughout America.

Now do you not appreciate what your blessed brother Harry Rogers did, in compiling from the Books and the Magazines the Group Outline, which the Great Divine Director asked us to use, that the activity might be uniform throughout America for this very identical accomplishment? It has been accomplished.

Precious Ones, will you not feel and allow a great deep gratitude to fill your Heart and world for this? To some of you it may sound like so many words. Oh, that you knew how much more it really means. Will you not accept — take advantage of this Opportunity; and with a greater earnestness, greater sincerity, and greater firmness, call the Great Intelligent Energy forth from your "Mighty I AM Presence" to act in you and your world and continue this Accomplishment with the speed of lightning? I tell you that it is possible at this point, if you will follow the directions I offer, to accomplish all with the speed of lightning.

Beloved Ones of Los Angeles, who have taken the initiative in much of the Call that has gone forth, it is very wonderful. Our blessed Mr. Sindelar! He has so untiringly worked to beautify and bring forth the wonderful material that has gone into the *Voice of the "I AM"*! How everyone in America should bless him. Within that blessed Brother are dissolving all human things, all human qualities. Each day more and more he is feeling the selflessness of that great Service which he chose to render, at the request of the Ascended Master Jesus. Such loyalty of Service is a Beacon-Light everywhere.

So also is the Service of you Group Leaders and beloved Students everywhere a Beacon-Light in that same great loyalty and selflessness. So too is the twenty-four hour Service which you are rendering of your own volition. Does it not show to the World what loyalty to the Light means? In that constant improvement and beauty of your mind, body, world, and the greater supply which is coming forth for you, is an eternal proof to all mankind of the Great Reality of this Great Stream of Light.

Today, oh, Beloved Ones, great is your privilege! Great is your Freedom, which stands with the Door wide open facing into the great Eternal Light which holds all things for you. Will you not accept It? Will you not continue? The Great "Presence" has pushed back the doors of doubt and fear, and over you is written in Golden Light — your Freedom. Will you not accept It? Enter in now with great firm determination, and see how quickly will all disturbance dissolve and disappear from your world.

You are now the master of your world if you will but accept and use your Dominion of the "Presence." Never question your ability, your authority, your power of achievement. God, the "Mighty I AM Presence," whose Ray of Light and Energy beats your Heart and sustains your Life is your certain Victory always. Will you not engrave that upon your consciousness for constant use, so It may show you and give you the eternal proof that you cannot fail? A little child when learning to walk falls down many times, but does it think anything about that? It gets up and tries again.

So today, if you have made mistakes, be not discouraged by it, but with a firmer determination arise and say: " 'Mighty I AM Presence,' see that I make no more mistakes! Take command of this mind and body! Stop this human activity that makes mistakes! Let Your Intelligence direct, Your Mighty Light protect, and hold me Invincible against any outside condition, suggestion, or anything else which would deprive me any longer of my Freedom and Victory."

Written above you in the Open Door and the Light of your "Presence" is your Victory. You have accomplished It now! Go forth! Look not to right nor left, but stand firm in the Glory of your "Mighty I AM Presence," until the fullness of It comes quickly into Action. It not only beautifies and perfects your body, but in It you stand firm, untouched by human suggestions of any kind.

When people come to you with discordant things, be silent. Then you will hold your world in this Great harmony, until the fullness of It looses the Power of the "Presence" to go forth and do what is required. No one thing is more difficult for mankind to conquer than the continual revolving in thought of some discordant thing, or continued—will you pardon the expression—"hashing over" with your acquaintances or friends, things that are discordant. Put them out of your Life and never refer to them if you want to be free. When one human tries to blame something on to another human, they are stifling their own progress. Remember that your Heart knows well enough whether you have made a mistake or not. If you have not, then anyone who says you have, cannot harm you. So remember that. Now again I say to you, the doors of doubt and fear are open, held back by the Hands of your "Mighty I AM Presence," and above you is Freedom. ENTER IN!

I say to the precious young people, Beloved Ones of the Light! Guard your world—your feeling world! Shun drink, intoxicants of every kind, excesses of every kind as you would a poisonous serpent. You have, in the Acknowledgment of your "Presence," the quick Open Door to your Freedom, if you govern your feeling world; but do not accept the vicious suggestions that come through the schools and colleges today, through the vicious activity which has entered into those wonderful places. Know that the Purity of your "Presence" is the only thing worthwhile in your world; then you will be able to hold your balance, go forth in the Call to your "Presence," and fill your world with the Perfection It holds for you. If you waste your energy, if you accept these tragic suggestions, then you will follow the trend of mankind and be in the limitations of the outer activity. Today you have the Knowledge in your hand, the Scepter in your hand, in the Name of the "Mighty I AM Presence," by which you can fill your world with Happiness, Beauty, Purity, and Perfection. I plead with you, *stand guard over your world!* Your "Presence" will, if called into Action!

Remember, you can love your friends more powerfully without your arms around them. Then you are not in danger of the human desires sweeping in and causing you to do things you will regret the rest of your Life. Oh, Beloved Precious Young People! I have watched the progress of mankind throughout the centuries, and have seen beautiful, blessed young men and women go down under the desires of the human and suggestions from the human that tell them they should waste their energy. Then in a few years they become decrepit and aged, when they could have maintained the youth, beauty, and perfection in their bodies, sustained by the conservation of that energy. Oh, you young people and you older people who have made mistakes! Call on the Law of Forgiveness! Take a firm, determined stand with the "Mighty I AM Presence" to hold control in your world, to take out of you all wrong desires, and to hold Its Dominion there forever.

Today, Beloved Ones, My Love enfolds you with the fullness of Its Power for your Happiness, Freedom, and Ascension. I pour forth the Great Love of the

Great Host of Ascended Masters, the Great Cosmic Beings, and the Legion of Light, to glorify, to enfold you and hold you within Its Mighty Radiance unto your Eternal Victory. The Glory of the Light of God, the "Mighty I AM Presence" within you, enfold you in Its Invincible Protection! Enfold you in Its Mighty Directing Intelligence, and clothe you in Its Mighty Light, forever sustained. I thank you.

GREAT DIVINE DIRECTOR'S
DISCOURSE

PAN PACIFIC CLASS — LOS ANGELES, CALIFORNIA

APRIL 4, 1937

GLORIFIED are all this day in the Sacred Radiance of the Great Cosmic Light which has come into action at Our bidding today, that you might have the benefit of Its Radiance in this concentrated Energy, Intelligence, and Activity. Out of the fullness of this Great Cosmic Light will come to humanity its Freedom! In your great Call to the Light, which is your "Mighty I AM Presence," you are fulfilling the requirements of the human octave of Life. Without that, the Great Cosmic Light would not be able, but in a small degree, to interfere with your Free Will. The Call of so many in America today has made it possible for this Blessing of the Great Cosmic Light to enter in the fullness of Its Power. To this end We hope for complete Freedom. The next few months will tell how much of the cataclysmic activity will be governed.

Unhappy Europe! Will you with Us visualize and call forth the Mighty Cosmic Light, the Assistance of the Great Legion of Light, the Great Host of Masters, and the Great Cosmic Beings, to stay the onrushing destruction there? Much depends upon your Call; Europe does not understand how. The great mass of the people have largely accepted the appearance. Therefore, I ask you to give your Call for the assistance of your fellowman there. You cannot imagine the Service you might render! In all the activity of the Messengers We have never once asked this, but tonight I ask it because it is needed.

There is a great volume of energy and Light released at the Call of more than two hundred thousand Students who are sending up their Call tonight, knowing this is the closing day of this Class, knowing of some of the great Radiance which is here. How grateful, how very grateful We are, who have waited so long for the attention of mankind to be drawn to these limitless Powers that could give them the Assistance required.

You today who are learning something of this Great Infinite Law, the Law of Life and Its Conscious Application, are privileged indeed. We—who have attained, have Our Freedom, and so long have been waiting for mankind to come to the point where this could come forth—are grateful for this Call. Otherwise, this would have been the greatest cataclysm which has ever come on Earth. We hope to minimize it, so the least possible destruction will occur. May the onrushing Cosmic Light produce Its Perfection for mankind, in and through them, untouched, uncolored by human, discordant creation. Many of you will live to see and experience the Great, Great Transformation! It is on Its way!

Tire not in giving your Mighty Decrees for the Freedom of the Earth! Know you not, oh, Precious Ones, that in the Call to the Light for the Freedom of America and the World, your Freedom is compelled to come forth because in this Call your thought and feeling are withdrawn from self? Do you know that intellectual vanity and self-pity are the greatest tragedies in the experience of mankind today? It takes away from the individual the recognition and acceptance of the Power of Light which beats each Heart, which gives each one the service he requires.

Tonight, Our Rejoicing is so very great, to be of Assistance; for the Service which it has been possible for Me to render since the Messengers were in San Francisco, I am very grateful and joyous to say, has been accomplished—because of your love, the love of the Students of Saint Germain. You shall, ere long, know what the Beloved Saint Germain has meant to you and the World!

To Him is due all credit for the bringing forth of this Wondrous Knowledge of the "Mighty I AM Presence" in Its purity, clearness, and simplicity. It cannot be misunderstood. Yet the majesty of Its Power is there. Behold It! Oh, Beloved Children of the Light, use It! Feel your authority in your Call to your "Mighty

I AM Presence" and waver not! Your Victory is sure through the Service which I have been able to render you, all Students in America, and those in the other parts of the World who are in touch with this Radiance! Do you know, have you thought how there are those already in touch with this Radiance in every nation in the World?

Quickly and surely there have gone forth these Wonderful Books, giving the Experience of this Beloved Brother standing before you. They are carrying this Light to the World. Into all parts of the World those Books have gone. Their Light carries them everywhere, and ere long they will reach hundreds of thousands and carry their Message of Light and Freedom to all.

Your Call, Beloved Ones, your Decrees have acted with almost Infinite Power. Do you realize what a blessing you are giving to the rest of mankind—you who have come to know the Glory and Freedom into which you have entered? As the Beloved Saint Germain told you today, oh, your Doorways are held back by your Mighty "Presence," because of your Call to It. Doubts and fears shall vanish from the Earth! I so decree it, that mankind may enter into the Glory of the Freedom which every Heart knows and one day will experience!

So We ask you to go on and on and on, into the greater and greater Light and Freedom. Arise! Awaken in the fullness of the Light of your "Presence," that your Light may shine and illumine the Earth; that you may pour forth such a Mighty Radiance from your "Mighty I AM Presence" that the very Radiance becomes visible to the human form! Then will mankind seek the Light, every one!

Weary not, oh, Beloved Ones who have called so earnestly for some definite manifestation of the proof of these Great Laws. Surely you have before you, so far as proof is concerned, every proof that any Heart can desire of the Reality of these Laws and Their Application. Yet shall your Call be answered more fully. Abide in patience. Your Call cannot be denied!

Remember, as your earnestness and intensity increase and the Light within you expands, it becomes compulsory for that Great Light to answer you, if your sincerity remains dauntless. You have in your hands —oh, that you might understand it fully—your Scepter of Power and Freedom! Apply It, oh, Beloved Ones, with all earnestness, giving no thought as to time or space; but just go on in the great joy of applying the Law of your "Presence." Let It do Its Perfect Work in Its own good time. See that the intellect and human impulses do not in any way interfere with the Glory of Its Expansion; for It will one day give you all the proof in the world that you want—or anyone else—of Its Efficiency, Its Power, Its Authority. So I ask you to be patient. Naught shall be withheld from anyone who has entered into this Freedom which just came! Make no mistake! It is no idle concept!

In the setting aside of this one-year period, it means one third of your Life-effort in this embodiment is set aside, glorifying you by an Assistance unheard of in the history of the Earth. It gives Assistance in dissolving and consuming your own creations, that you may more quickly enter into the Freedom of the Light which beats your Heart — the "Mighty I AM Presence." May you all feel the importance of these Words.

I speak as One having Authority — all Authority — human, Divine, and Cosmic! Therefore, you shall see the Fulfillment of My Words! According to the earnestness and intensity with which you continue to adore your "Mighty I AM Presence," call It forth into action, and hold harmony in your feelings, will this come quickly or yet be delayed.

The Messengers are pleading with you, with all the Students everywhere, for the need of harmony maintained in your feelings, of purity of thought and feeling. Then the Great Law can come forth quickly and do Its Work. You, Precious Ones, humanly your part is to make the Call, stand by with firm determination, and allow the Great Power of Infinite Light to flow forth through you and into your world to do Its Perfect Work, Its Mighty Process of Creation.

No longer does the power of darkness control mankind. Today it has lost its power. Tomorrow you shall enter through your Gates of Freedom! To the degree that you can feel the Truth of My Words and feel It active within you, shall It be quickly or otherwise manifest. This is for you individually as well as the Nation. As the great Decrees go forth continuing their mighty Work, and with the Assistance of this great Light, will the Earth send forth its praise and rejoicing. Even the rocks shall tremble with the Joy of Freedom; even the trees and the vegetation shall lift themselves in rejoicing.

Such is the Power that awaits the Earth. You, oh, Precious Ones, are responsible because of your willingness to stand the impact of human thought and feeling, your willingness to go on in the acceptance of your "Presence" in spite of the ridicule of the ignorant. In that Call you have enabled this Great Light to come forth—this Great Transcendent Blessing to enter within the Earth. Feel Its Glory, Its expanding Light which will bring forth Freedom, Happiness, and every good thing.

As the Earth enters through this into its own once again, then all shall have all required for use. All human selfishness shall be wiped from the Earth forever. Then will there be released by that Light, more than mankind's fondest imagination has ever conceived, even more by far. Can you not, will you not live in this great, great anticipation, until you see the fulfilling of Its Glory?

How privileged you are to be a part of the great vanguard which is enabling this to be done. Oh, Precious Ones, do you in your outer activity sometimes feel humble because of your lack of something? Then I say to you: Arise! Awaken! Stand forth in the Light of your "Mighty I AM Presence," and allow Its Power to take out of you that feeling! Feel your authority and power in the acceptance of your "Presence" to let this Light flow forth to bless, heal, prosper, and enlighten all with whom you come in contact, and flood the Earth with Its Purity and Perfection. Mankind being the creator of all that has limited the Earth and yourself, then in that great Call shall come the release. Even the Earth shall find itself again rejoicing in the Glory of this Freedom, as well as yourselves.

Today will you not rejoice with Me, with all of Us? Enter again into great calm serenity in the sending forth of your Decrees, individually and in your Groups, that the Perfect Mighty Work of the "Presence" may go forth filling the Earth with Its Beauty and Perfection. I rejoice with you with all My Heart that there are so many of mankind today whose Light has expanded enough to allow them to recognize their "Presence."

Once they gaze upon that amazing Chart, they know they have come home once again. In that, they know and enter into the Glory of Its Application. This causes the Great Light from within to expand and expand until every cell of the body becomes a glowing, blazing Sun of Light. Oh, Precious Ones, will you not believe Me when I say it is possible for many of you sitting here in this room to shortly call forth the Light to expand in every cell of your body, until everyone about you can see that Light with his physical eyes? There are five in this room whom I could place My Hand upon and expand that Light, until every one of you would see the Glory of It. I say this for your encouragement. Will you not let this Light expand?

In the great calm serenity and the fullness of the Great Power which is the Light within you, you have the Reward It brings. Let no one, yourself or anyone else, longer limit you in the Acknowledgment of your "Presence"! If you do, the fault is yours. Remember, nothing binds you but yourself. There is no power in Heaven or Earth to bind you longer but yourself!

In the fullness of My Love and Light I bless you, oh, Precious Ones. Today you have become a part of My Love! As those Beloved Children in India became a part of My Love, so today you have become a part of My Love! God bless you! Feel Its Wondrous Embrace enfold you and sustain you forever with Its Courage, Strength, and Infinite Directing Wisdom, Its full Power to act.

"Mighty I AM Presence" of each one, I charge through the Higher Mental Body of each one the

Activity of My Presence and Power of Divine Love, to do Its Perfect Work for these beloved ones of the Light. I call forth the Mighty Violet Consuming Flame to dissolve and consume quickly every vestige of human creation. Will you join Me in this Call in the silence and sacredness of your Heart, that Its Service and Assistance may be given without limit?

I leave with you the Blessings of the Great Ascended Masters, the Legion of Light, and the Great Cosmic Beings. Remember, the Great Silent Watcher has His Eye upon you! No longer may the Students of the Light practice any deception. Wise are they who always tell the Truth. Accept tonight My Eternal Enfolding Love, Light, Wisdom, and Power to hold you in Its Embrace until your full Victory and Ascension. I thank you.

OUR BELOVED REX'S
DISCOURSE

CORPORONS' LONG BEACH GROUP

APRIL 5, 1937

BELOVED Ones of California, it is My Great Joy to speak a few Words to you from My Heart and to remind you that not so many years ago I visited your city with My father. Does it seem incredible to you that so much could have taken place in such a few years? Think, since this Beloved Brother came into Our home in Wyoming, the Heavens have opened and We have entered into Our Real Home in Its fullness!

We thought Our mother had passed on, like most people are supposed to do. Yet after this Good Brother's entrance in Our home, We too discovered she had been Free all those years. We sometimes thought that she was possibly in the tomb where her body was placed. Then Beloved Saint Germain came to My father, explained all, and began the Instruction which so quickly set him free from the human world and activity.

Beloved Ones, feel with Me tonight, oh, how Real, how very Real is this Mighty "Presence" which beats your Hearts. In your sincere, firm determination, holding your attention upon the "Presence," everything can and will dissolve and disappear from you and your world which has held you bound in any way. The "Presence" is doing it now, oh, Precious Ones! It is doing it with great speed.

We are so grateful that you have established a Reading Room in your city. It has been made a Mighty Focus of Light. Give your full support to it. Beloved Ones, in your Call to your "Presence," never miss one day calling your "Presence" into Action to bless that Reading Room. Pour forth Its All-expanding Power and Light, which the Great Ones have drawn there tonight. Let it be an ever-expanding Activity to spread the Radiance of the "Presence" in and through your city, to touch hundreds of those whose Light has expanded sufficiently for them to accept this Understanding of the "Mighty I AM Presence" and have the Blessing which It brings.

You will notice, Beloved Ones, that there is not a single part of this Understanding which Saint Germain has brought forth that interferes with anything in the World. It is just the Glorious Acknowledgment of the Source of your Life, of all lives. It is all Power acting in your world, taking command, holding Its Dominion, producing Its Perfection there, forever sustained; and in your power of qualification, Beloved Ones, assert this. Oh, that I might cause you to feel now the power which is within you to assert It! Assert this Dominion of your "Presence"! Feel It deeply, until no longer a single human thing touches your world to cause you to waver for an instant.

You know, under the Radiance of Saint Germain We entered so quickly into the Glorious Radiance of Our "Presence" that We really had not time for anything else to come. It is really very wonderful. Even today, We continue to marvel at the speed with which Our Freedom came to Us, after this Blessed Brother came into Our home. He is in your home. Do you realize that? In your home—for your home is your world, and your world surrounds you! Do you realize that, Dear Ones?

The greatest home in the World is the home that surrounds you, because that is the only home you can live in. You may live in buildings, but that is not always your home, even though you may own it from the human standpoint. Unless the Glory and Harmony in the Understanding of your "Presence" is there, is it home? Tell Me! Is it home, unless there is the Harmony of the "Presence" within it?

Therefore, I call your attention to this tonight to remind you that your home is your world which surrounds your human form, the only world in which you can ever live. If you will realize this and then, in the Acknowledgment of your "Presence," fill your world with the blazing, dazzling Light of the "Presence," then do you not see, if you are in a physical home—a building—the Radiance from your "Presence" will fill that home because It knows no obstruction or interference? If you will think of your home in that way, I am sure you will find enormous blessing and benefit.

I think you might be interested in knowing something of what We have been doing since this Good Brother returned from Chananda's Home in India. We spent four and a half months in Chananda's Home after his return. Then We returned to the Retreat in Arabia where the greatest, most magnificent Understanding of the use of the Light Rays is given forth. As all of Us just naturally selected the use of the Light Rays for the Work We were to do, We returned there to receive further Instruction.

You would possibly think that My imagination were running riot if I were to tell you the Accomplishment from that time to this, in Our ability to utilize, to direct, to wield those Powers which come from the use of the Light Rays. We are still just lads yet, you know; and yet We are able to do things today, Precious Ones, that seem absolutely incredible to the human sense. I say this tonight to carry forth the Radiance of the Truth of Our Accomplishment into your mental and feeling world, that you may feel the Power of Our Activity in your feeling world—because remember, your feeling world is your Powerhouse. Unless you do get the full consciousness of a thing into your feeling, you are only having partial results; and that is the trouble with mankind today. Individuals still unknowingly keep trying to do a thing with the human intellect, which is not the Knower — never was! never will be! because the Heart is the True Knower, and the full Power of the "Presence" is anchored in the Heart.

When the intellectual activity is backed up by the Feeling of the Truth from the Heart and intensified by It, then the intellect can be a remarkable servant. This is why tonight I endeavor to charge into your feeling world the confidence, the conviction of your power to release from your "Presence" at your Call and anchor within your feeling world, certain Qualities which it is My Privilege to pour forth. How? Through the very Projection of these Light Rays which We have learned how to use.

Beloved Ones, if you once knew the power that exists within your feeling world through the activity of your attention, you would leave the floor in the magnificence of that sudden realization, because momentarily you would sever the pull of Earth! One day in the Retreat in Arabia when We were tremendously in earnest — in fact We had become so intense upon the acquirement of what was before Us and its use, that four times We suddenly found Our feet at least three feet above the floor. We were standing there in the atmosphere, just as firm as We had stood a few moments before on the floor. This is how with intense attention to a specific thing, and to the extent that you have forgotten your form — does it cause the Earth to lose all attraction for your body. Then you will notice the moment your attention comes back, you settle down again.

This activity, through the attention, is what is going on in the feeling and outer activity of mankind right along. You are raising. In your recent Class, for instance, you were raised to a Tremendous Height. Again through your power of attention, in most instances as soon as you come back and touch the outer world's activity, you begin to accept its limitations; and unknowingly these act in the feeling body — the old habits to which you have been accustomed.

Here is a point We have found to be of great Assistance to Ourselves. Say: " 'Mighty I AM Presence,' take Eternal Command of my power of qualification. Do not let the old concepts or habit any longer have power in my world!" If you will do that, you will find it very helpful.

As We went on and on, We found there are those in the World, I am sorry to say, who have wholly destructive desires. We must counteract those desires among mankind. There was only within the last three months, one serving the destructive forces who conceived an idea of a partial use of the Ray — one of the Rays — that was very destructive. Of course the Ascended

Masters are watching over the World and They know immediately when anything of that kind is attempted. It had to be forestalled. It was My Joy, Privilege, and Service to act in that capacity!

Today, Beloved Ones, you are coming into an Activity which has for long periods existed on Venus. Notice! We are children yet, so to speak, and hope We always shall be; but think of it: Bob, Pearl, Nada, and I are no older than these beloved children here [Don and Marjory]. Yet We have use today of these Great Powers. In this Service which I was able to render is a Joy that is boundless; for it makes Me realize that in the Service which I am later to render in the outer world, It will continue to intensify Its Activity until one day when I come into the outer world and meet many of you, that same Power, that same Activity will be there. This is why a few moments ago I said to you, if you knew the power which you have for use in your feeling world by the power of your attention, Precious Ones, you would set yourselves free almost in one mighty sweep.

This is why the Beloved Messengers have recently called your attention to the necessity of saying so powerfully, so firmly, to all appearances, "You have no power!" Remember, Precious Ones, nothing in the World has any power except what you give it, so far as you are concerned or your world is concerned. Therefore anything that harms or limits you, to it you gave your Life which enables it to act — to come back and do that to you. Please get this firmly in your consciousness tonight. If you will do as I request, you will find a sense of Freedom never experienced before. There is no one in the World who would not absolutely set his foot down on such limitations, in firm determination, if he really understood that it is his own Life going into a thing which comes back and harms him. Otherwise it could not act. No discord or limitation could reach into anyone's world except through his own Life. I am sure you will get this into your consciousness tonight as never before. When you see an appearance out here of limitation, if that comes back to you as a limitation, then your Life is feeding it to limit or bring disturbance to you.

Then you will say: "Now then, we are getting down to Reality. If that be the case, I shall no longer feed my Life into anything to come back and harm me." This is just what all humanity has been doing. Individuals have blamed everything else but themselves for the conditions. The Truth is, they were feeding their own Life into the things which were actually limiting them and causing disturbance. Without the Stream of their Life it could not touch their world. Do you not see that?

Tonight, Beloved Ones, I shall anchor the Understanding of this within your consciousness. It will stand there active, for constant use. It will always remind you of Its Activity when you suddenly begin to accept that something has power to harm or limit you in the outer world.

You will stop right there and say: "Oh, no you don't! You did once, but you are not going to do it any more! You are not going to use my Life to harm me! 'Mighty I AM Presence,' take command! Cut this off and see that I no longer accept these appearances as having any power!" Do you not feel that as I am speaking it, it does enter into your feeling world now to act there with full power?

"No longer shall any appearance have any power from my Life unless it expresses Perfection. Knowing that only from the 'Presence' can come Perfection, then my attention shall go to my 'Presence'; and through my attention, there shall release from my 'Presence' everything I require in my outer world of activity. Knowing that my 'Presence' is my Intelligence, my Love, my Light, my Power to act, then to my 'Presence' alone will I give all Power, and not to human appearances. I am reminded that every time I give my attention to a limiting appearance or destructive activity, my Life is feeding it, and I certainly do not do so any more."

Do you realize, Beloved Ones, that this very Consciousness will forever make you alert? It will keep you prompted any time you start to give your attention to old habits and limiting or disturbing things. You will be prompted instantly: "No sir, you do not do it!" You will be surprised to find how alert you become. Now mark you, this alertness is the Selective Intelligence from your Higher Mental Body. Precious Ones, notice this! Your Higher Mental Body is still limited, so far as you are concerned, unless you give It the full Power to act.

Now then, by your refusing to give power any longer to appearances which are harmful or disturbing, it is just as if your Wall of Light says, "No! So far and no farther!" Then your Wall of Light is held firm to refuse acceptance to those appearances. Your Wall of Light stands there unyielding and impenetrable. When you call to your "Presence," there is nothing which rushes in to disturb the outflow of your "Mighty I AM Presence" to perform Its Mighty Service.

Believe Me, Beloved Ones, do not give any consideration to who you have been, or anything about it. If you begin to wonder who you were and accept that you were this, that, or the other thing in some other embodiment, you are dividing your attention. Instead give your attention to the "Presence" to fill your mind, body, and world with the Perfection which the "Presence" holds. It is the same thing, Dear Ones, as when you keep giving your attention to appearances that are of the outer world's activity.

You begin to go back into the activity of the lives in which you have lived, with which you are not concerned today. *It is not what you have been, but what you are today that counts!* So watch out that you do not fall into this habit of thought and feeling; for it limits you and takes the energy which you need to make the Call to the "Presence" and to enable It to flow out into your world, to produce your Perfect Activity, and to give you Power to achieve freedom here and now.

Saint Germain is the most Marvelous Being in the world, and His practical Application of the Law in the manner in which He gives Assistance to the Students is a most unparalleled thing. He will not allow His Students to give their attention to what they have been before, if they want to be free. Just as long as you keep feeding your Life, through the attention, into that which you have been, you cannot be what you desire today. See that?

Today is the important thing. What you have been is past and gone. Only to the extent that you call on the Law of Forgiveness for mistakes made, and use the Violet Consuming Flame to set you free from your human creations brought forth thus far, are you actually accomplishing the things required. However, you will not do this if you keep feeding your Life, through your attention, back into what you have been before. Your former Life has not a thing to do with what you are today.

I would not give a snap of My finger whether I was a prince, a king, a sheep herder—or what I was in the past, because when you come to the point of the Acknowledgment of your "Presence," then you have entered into your Eternal Stream of Freedom. There is nothing that can interfere with your Victory so long as you refuse to give your Life to discordant appearances, through your attention.

There have been any number of people who have, because of the unusualness of it, begun to look back, and thus enter into the vibratory action of embodiments in which they have lived in the past; and their entire attention was taken off the Glory of their Victory. Now that is why, Dear Ones, tonight I call your attention to this, because there are some of the Students who unknowingly are dropping into such habits. I plead with you, do not do it!

Give your whole attention, your whole Life to the "Presence," that It may again return Its Energy to you, intensified with the feeling of Its Perfection and Purifying Activity. As you do that, Beloved Ones, you will find such Glory filling your mind and body. On this particular point, do you know Saint Germain is adamant? He says, "Do not dare give your attention to any of Us before you give it to your 'Presence.' " This correct attitude is a most wonderful thing, because after all, your "Presence" is you!

It is All-powerful. Even We bow to the Majesty of the "Presence" of you who have not yet Ascended, because your "Presence" knows exactly what you require — I mean through your Higher Mental Body. The "Presence" of an unascended being is not cognizant of the requirements down here, but that one's Higher Mental Body is. It knows your requirements and needs, therefore answers full and completely if your attention is not divided.

Will you not accept this tonight, Precious Hearts, with the fullest cooperative power, and call your Higher Mental Body into action to seize and hold your attention on Perfection? Call to your "Presence" to use Its Mighty Discriminating Intelligence to stand Guard over you. Every time you start to feed your Life into some appearance out here, It will prompt you like that [quick wave of hand]. Then if you say, "Oh no, no more of that!" you will be surprised how quickly you can reverse those activities and bring your attention back to the "Presence," to prevent your Life going out into a scattering activity and acceptance of appearances that come before you. You have no idea how powerful this is.

I tell you, Precious Ones, if you were to see the energy that you feed into appearances in twelve hours of the waking state, you could scarcely believe it. Now just think what it means when you become imbued with anger, intense criticism, or some intense feeling which releases a volume of energy in one sweep. Do you not see, Dear Ones, how you are just throwing your Life away and scattering it broadcast to do no good for yourself or anyone else? If you allow your feeling to catapult anger, criticism, condemnation, or impurity of thought, do you not see how you intensify the same activity in someone else of mankind and make it hard for that one to gain his Victory? You are absolutely wasting, completely wasting your own Life energy through such feelings — scattering it broadcast without soil to grow in, except when it strikes qualities of a discordant kind. Then you are making it hard for someone else in that one's endeavor to attain the Victory.

Now you see your responsibility to your fellowman, to your assistants, those you love. When you do such things, you are depriving yourselves constantly of the Life energy which you require for your accomplishment or upon whatever your attention may be fixed.

Dear Hearts, I am grateful, very grateful for your alertness tonight and that which you are anchoring within your world for constant use, through your feeling. I know positively that you are going forth from this room tonight filled with a Consciousness of your Victory which you have never had yet. Now do not misunderstand Me. I do not consider that is due to Me, but to your acceptance of the Quality of the Truth which is spoken.

Watch out! Stand guard! Be alert, you Precious Ones, and do not allow any more of your energy to go forth to feed destructive things, through the power of your attention! Hold your energy, turn it back to the "Presence" and say: " 'Mighty I AM Presence,' flood me and my world with the Glory of Your Perfection. Sustain It with Your Directing Intelligence, with Your Power of Achievement." As you call Its Power into action you will feel a Glory—not a temporary thing, but an intensified, constantly increasing activity, called forth into action in your world, which will glorify you with a happiness and strength that you were not aware was there.

Notice! Your "Presence" is the Power acting. Whatever the condition is in your physical body or appearance has nothing to do really with the Ability of your "Presence." Your Call is everything. Your refusing to accept appearances which would be limiting is your power of assistance to the "Presence"; for that is all It requires to release the Fullness of Its Power and Action to produce Perfection in you and your world.

So tonight, in the Glory of the Freedom which is yours, in the Acknowledgment of your "Presence," which is the Governor of the Universe, will you not keep yourselves reminded of these simple Truths which are so majestic in action? Allow Them to come forth in your world and produce Perfection for you by no longer feeding your Life into any discordant thing — any limiting thing.

Old habit, Dear Ones, is a thing that has to be conquered. You can quickly reverse all those habits which have taken your energy, if you will. Remember, when you call your "Presence" into action to reverse these activities, the "Presence" will do it; but you must do your part in refusing to give your attention and Life, through your attention, into these things. Do you not see how absolutely logical and practical it is? It gives you such freedom in your feeling world.

Bob, Pearl, and Nada are present with Me, and are pouring out Their Great Love upon you. They have been, all the time I have been talking. You know, I am very happy to say that My sister, Nada, has taken on many of the Qualities of the Beloved Lady Master Nada, whose picture is in the Magazine. She made Her Ascension some 2,700 years ago. In Our Association with Them, it is amazing how quickly one takes on those Qualities. As you learn to hold yourself free from discordant appearances, then They can more quickly pour into your world that which makes you like Them.

There is one more point I want to leave with you tonight, Beloved Ones: In your attention to the Ascended Masters, who have gone every step of the way that you must go — and your attention has been given so marvelously — They can fill you and your world with the Quality which They are. In this way My sister, Nada, has taken on from the Lady Master Nada, the Qualities which She has caused to become so powerful in Her World.

First, give your Acknowledgment to the "Presence." Then if you need courage and strength that you do not seem quite able to call forth, turn your attention to Saint Germain, Jesus, Nada, the Divine Director, or some of the other Ascended Ones — Cha Ara, Chananda, or some of those Blessed Ones. They will come back to you, because Their Attention is again upon the Consciousness of that which accomplishes Perfection. Therefore, It must flow into your world to do for you whatever you require. Do you not see how perfectly practical all of that is? There is not anything impractical about any of It.

We try repeatedly to bring to your attention certain things and show you definitely how you can right now begin to govern your world. Refuse to give attention to appearances which have disturbed you, and give all your attention to your "Presence."

Now do you not see how that which is known as doubt and fear could not affect you or your world unless you feed your energy into it? That is your qualification. Your Life goes out and becomes charged with fear to come back and disturb you; or it goes out and is charged with doubt, which comes back and causes you to doubt.

Do you not see how—right now—you are master of your world and the governing activity which controls those qualities and prevents them any longer entering into your Life or world? It is the most practical thing anyone could conceive, and it is within the use of any person who will apply it, but you must be alert. You cannot, Dear Ones, just let your feelings run riot. You must call the "Presence" into action and refuse any longer to give attention to things out here. Wherever your Life flows, it not only gives action, but must bring back its effect upon you sooner or later.

Tonight, in the fullest Power of the Ascended Host, I ask Them to anchor within your feeling world the full Power of every Word that has been spoken here, to make this practical; to give you the full consciousness of your ability to control, through the power of your attention, all of these activities which have taken your Life energy or given it a power to disturb or limit you. That no longer has any power!

"Mighty I AM Presence!" I issue that Decree for these beloved ones tonight. Stand guard over their attention! Hold their attention in control, conscious control, that they no longer feed their Life into any limiting, discordant, destructive activity to come back and touch their world! Stand guard, "Mighty I AM

Presence," over the attention of each one and hold it upon Thee! See that it is always held upon Thee and Thy Perfection! Supply their worlds with everything that they require—and in abundance! The "Presence" is not limited, and in the Light which beats your Heart—which is Self-luminous, Intelligent Substance—is all that you require.

Today you have entered into the Activity of the Mighty Cosmic Light—or rather yesterday—and you have Assistance heretofore unknown. Will you not accept it? In this humble, simple Explanation I have given tonight, will you not remember it and remind yourselves often that your attention must be to your "Presence"? Every time it tries to go to something outside, say: "Stop! I will have no more of that. You obey the Law of your 'Presence'—put your attention there! Then my world will have the Power, the Perfection which my 'Presence' is. I refuse any longer to give my attention to anything else! Therefore, there is nothing can longer enter into my world but that Perfection which is the 'Presence'!"

Out of the Eternal Light and Thy Glory, oh, "Mighty I AM Presence," We accept tonight the fullness of Thy Active Presence, Thy Eternal Guard about each one—that their attention may be held firmly upon Thee with absolute refusal to let it act anywhere else. Therefore, It releases over all of them a constant Stream of Thy Almighty Energy, bringing

Perfection, Happiness, Health, and everything good into the world of each one, forever sustained. I thank you.

OUR BELOVED NADA'S
DISCOURSE

RATANA'S HOLLYWOOD GROUP — HOLLYWOOD, CALIFORNIA

APRIL 6, 1937

TODAY, O Beloved Ones, is a cherished moment for Me, so recently have I attained the Victory and Freedom from human limitations. It is such a great Joy to convey to you the Feeling We have in this really Great Achievement. Think of it! Precious Ones, this Eternal Goal is Freedom forever from all the human has gone through in the many, many centuries in which We have all lived.

One can scarcely realize where We stood so few years ago when this Good Brother came into Our home. How little did We dream then of what was to follow. I say to you with all sincerity and earnestness: Right now, you stand in the same position! How little do you know, as We did then, what is just before you in your Achievement. Will you not join with Me in accepting the Limitless Power of your "Presence" to do this same thing for you? We did not know, any more than you do today what is before you. If one had told Us, even the day this Good Brother arrived in Our home, all that would take place, We probably

302

would have said it was incredible and impossible.

Our Example stands before you, Beloved Ones, in Its Infinite Power to strengthen, encourage, and allow you to feel this—the same Great Victory—is yours. Unless you allow your human feelings, through your attention and qualification, to have domination within you longer, then you too will go forth as We did. There is no mistake about it. Everything depends upon the control of your feeling world. You do have the Authority; and now, in the Acknowledgment of the "Presence," you have the Power to achieve your Victory.

In Our home We thought Our training was a private activity; but you are having almost identically the same Instruction, as It is being given to you today, through the intensified Power and Radiance of the Great Ones. We did not know the Goal any more than you do today. Yet it was accomplished.

Through Our humble Effort, We try to bring you greater Feeling of your Self-control and Mastery of your feelings, and keep it sustained. We endeavor to give you the same Feeling which We have now through Our Achievement. Then you will see how real, how very tangible is Our Assistance, which is now being given you.

The Great Ones have said to Us that in the Enthusiasm and Joy of Our Attainment—and still having a certain connection with the Earth which I may not explain to you just now — We are able to pour a Radiance, a Strength into your feeling world, which sometimes Those far Greater than Ourselves are not permitted to do. There is some of this Explanation which I am not permitted to give you; but I can explain enough to give you the incentive, the feeling and Power to stand firm — very firm in the Acknowledgment of your "Presence." We can give you the full feeling of your authority and ability right now to achieve any given goal upon which your attention may be fixed.

Some of you have had a certain achievement in your outer activities previous to this Understanding of the "Presence." I want to say to you, today you have a thousand times greater power to go forth Victorious than you had three years ago. Is not that something to think about? To think that in three years you have gone ahead, as it were, like a rocket! Oh, there may not seem to be so great a change as yet in the outer; but, oh, Beloved Ones, if you saw from the Inner Standpoint how great your achievement has been, your courage would be boundless.

Now notice, as the Messengers have said, in the Acknowledgment of your "Presence" is everything! I mean all activity comes from within, out. In your previous understanding, you thought you had to gather all things from without, in. That activity is just the reverse of what it ought to be. All things come from within, out. Therefore, the greater part of your achievement is accomplished before you become much aware of it in the outer activity.

It was so with My mother, even when she thought she was really passing on. One day she said to Us that she thought she was passing. When We thought she had become unconscious—and she had, to human sense—she went out from her body with Saint Germain's Assistance, and was receiving Instruction from Him as to what to do. He told her to allow her body to be placed in the tomb because of the requirement of the outer law which still held sway at the time. You see, in previous times during the achievement of these things, the outer world was not permitted to know the Inner Activity which was going on. That outer condition still held sway at the time of My mother's attainment. We grieved so deeply. Oh, today I think how foolish it was; but We were serious. We thought her passing a real tragedy, and many people do today. Dear Hearts, We assure you, as the Great Messengers have—there is no such thing as death in the world, in the Universe. You simply change your form for a finer one; but still there is no death anywhere.

Oh, the relief, the release! Precious Saint Germain made it possible, in the Cave of Symbols, for Our precious mother to come to Us in Her tangible Body, lowering the rate of Her Ascended Body to make it

visible to Us. She held Us again in Her arms. Oh!
is there anything in the world so Victorious, so
Wonderful as that? We had thought so long through
Our previous training that death was real, although
My mother knew years before that it was not, and
tried very delicately to assure Us that there was no
death. Yet We did not comprehend it, even with all
that she put forth. Today We know it is not real, for
there is no death anywhere in the Universe. If you
can believe that We are truthful, then you will accept this and set yourselves free from any such thought
ever again.

Oh, the Joy which comes from that definite feeling! Grief seems so real at the time. Yet there is no
need of one tear in the whole world. Mankind should
understand that to generate grief is but to destroy
oneself! Those who understand the "I AM Presence"
can call forth Its Great Joy. Your Higher Mental
Body already knows all these Great Truths. Then
do you not see, Precious Ones, this Law is not something really new to you, for your Higher Mental Body
knows of It already? We but call your attention to
certain things to awaken a response within you; and
Our Feeling, pouring into your feeling world, releases
into your outer use that which you already know
within. Everyone in his feeling world knows of this
Truth; some have called forth fragments of It. No
one in the World, even in the time of Jesus, ever

brought forth such clear, simple, Majestic, All-powerful Knowledge of the "Mighty I AM Presence" as Saint
Germain has brought forth. The Law of the World
at that time did not permit it. Jesus knew It, and so
did the Disciple John; but others did not know and
comprehend. Jesus did not talk as freely with the other
Disciples as He did with John the Beloved; for he
understood all that Jesus was going to do, but the
others did not.

So it is today. As the Light within each one expands
sufficiently, then will the individual have definitely
the clear Understanding of various points as they come
along. In this endeavor to convey some of these practical Truths to you, My Comprehension will act within
your feeling world, because My Feeling is yours while
I am talking to you.

You never in all your Life heard tell of such Happiness as Pearl, Rex, Bob, and I are having. Everything, every movement, every new achievement comes
as wondrous, wondrous, enthusiastic Joy. We never
think about getting tired or feeling limited in any
sense. We just go on and on and on, in the Wondrous Expansion of the Light, pouring forth through
those Great Light Rays which you see about the
"Presence." We have been able to enter into Its
Great Radiance and project these Rays to do many
wonderful things, which such a short time ago We
could not have imagined. This is why I say to you,

Beloved Ones, do not let your human intellect or feeling limit you one moment longer. Every time a thought of limitation of any kind comes to your attention, simply say to it: "Now you stop right there! You have no power! You are not going to take my Life anymore to feed any human sense of limitation!" and it has to disappear. Do you see?

Rex said this to you last night — I felt really proud of Him. This is the point you need to remember, Dear Hearts, to understand: Everything you give power to through your attention, to limit or harm you, is your own Life doing it. Is not that an astounding thing? Think! All through these centuries, we have fed our very Life into things to harm and limit us! Well, as our beloved Donald says, "Its day is done!" It is, if you will assert it! Do you not see this? If you will assert your Power of the "Presence," and mean it, to all those appearances — their day *is* done so far as their ability to limit you is concerned, because they cannot have your Life any longer by which to do it!

Oh, every day, more and more practical, clear, and simple is this Understanding becoming to you, as you see how every movement and activity of your consciousness during the day in the waking state, you have been using these powers, but without understanding. Now that you do understand what their activity has been doing within and about you, you will not allow your Life to feed any more energy into the things which limit or disturb you. Will you not please hold this firm in your consciousness for constant use? Because, oh, so quickly, even as quickly as We did, you can be free.

Think of it, Beloved Ones, beginning tomorrow with this Great Activity and Release of the Cosmic Light, there is being given the greatest Assistance mankind has ever had to free themselves from all human limitations, and to enter right now, today, into the steady—notice this—the steady, sure Activity of the Ascension.

As I look into your Hearts, while these Words are being flashed before this Beloved Messenger, and I see the ability within you, can you imagine My Feeling and My Determination to quicken, awaken, and bring forth into action that which I know and see to be there within you? Now, We shall not give any more quarter to the human accumulation. It has no power to limit you any longer!

I congratulate our beloved Donald and Marjory in the recent determined stand they have taken for the Victory. If they will just hold steady to that, how quickly they can be free!

In many of you precious ones, and in many of these beloved young people in whose Groups We have been pouring forth Our Love and Radiation, We see within your Hearts the Expansion of your

Light—far beyond that of which the outer is aware. Such Achievement is before you! With Purity in thought and feeling maintained, and with refusal of acceptance of any discordant thing to act in your feeling world, you would go forward like a rocket, as We did, into this Great Achievement, the Ascension—your Freedom—the Goal of all human pilgrimage on Earth.

Today, oh, Beloved Ones, you stand within the Gates of Freedom! I urge you to contemplate often the picture of *The Open Door*. This marvelous picture that Mr. Brooks of New York brought forth is really a very marvelous thing, because it does give you the exact eye picture of your "Presence" called forth into Action, holding back forever the doors of doubt and fear. As you contemplate it with a firm stand for your freedom, saying to all appearances, "You have no power!" do you not see how it makes the completed activity for your own freedom? We all rejoice in the sure, definite intensity with which you are feeling and bringing into use these Great Powers which you have always had, and which flow into your Heart from the "Presence." Each day, as all of this becomes more practical, more real to you, will find that you can assert yourself. You can issue a Decree and find it very quickly fulfilled.

Bob, Rex, Pearl, and Myself, so often since We arrived in Arabia, have discussed this so many, many times. Hardly do We enter into a discussion until this point is brought forth: Our Great Gratitude to Our Beloved Saint Germain for having taught Us in the beginning that the Great Law does not permit the waste of this great Energy which flows through from the "Presence." We accepted that. We lived in obedience to the Law. Do not—through anger, sex, or any other condition—waste your energy! Saint Germain's explanation to Us was Law, and We lived and abided in It. Therefore We entered very quickly into the Great Perfection which the "Presence" is, and which everyone can have.

Let Me remind you again today, Precious Ones, that all mankind has made mistakes; and the great Understanding of calling on the Law of Forgiveness is a most wonderful, wonderful thing. You do not realize the full importance of it, as We see this Activity. We have watched certain individuals who were very intense in calling on the Law of Forgiveness for any mistakes which have ever been made. You do not have to know what they are; but as We see the effect of their calling in their feeling world—well, it is just stupendous! I want you to know the action of these various things which are within your use. It is so easily done! You can have, oh, the great, great Victory quickly!

Think of it! All through the centuries mankind has looked upon Jesus as a Special Being, and thought,

"Well, no one else can attain the Ascension because He was a Special Being." Yet He said in His own Words, "All these things shall ye do and greater things shall ye do." Yet mankind has clothed Him with a condition which they felt it was never possible to reach. That was the great, great mistake of humanity. He spoke the Truth to the whole living world; and all things that He did, mankind shall do! They have to do the same!

The Great Cosmic Light today comes into the Earth and compels you now, whether you will or not, to understand this. The Cosmic Light compels the Expansion of your own Light and you become more sensitive. Do not begin to feel that you are imposed upon—you have to be! Accept the sensitiveness to It, for you have the Power of the "Presence" in Self-control. Then you will govern any sensitiveness, and it will be a Blessing untold to you.

If you give way, through your power of qualification, and say you are becoming so sensitive you cannot move in the outer world, then you are undoing all the Perfection which can come to you and is there for you. You see all these things are so practical. Yet through human qualification, individuals often undo the things that they might otherwise accomplish. You are master of your attention, your power of qualification, and your vision. You may look upon two automobiles which come together on the road.

You can look upon such an activity without accepting it into your world. Take your firm stand on all such things in your cities where you often see those occurrences. Issue the Decree: " 'Mighty I AM Presence!' Stand guard over my *feeling world*! Enable me to look upon things without accepting their discord into my *feeling world.*" This is what you can do.

That is what this Good Brother does, and is the reason why all the silly, untruthful reports made about him do not touch him. They cannot affect him; but Heaven help the person who does it, because it has to go back to the individual who sends it out. So it is with you. There cannot a thing enter your world unless you accept it. We want to fix this in your consciousness forever.

You know, so much has been given us by Our Great and Blessed Saint Germain! If you could see how He has poured out this Light like a mighty river, ever since the Messengers started out and came to you, your Heart would rejoice. It has just poured like a river, and I do not wonder that you do not hold clearly before you some of the simpler things which are acting in your world every day. You have come to the point now where you must become cognizant of the simple things which you thought possibly were not of importance, but it is the little things achieved that make the Great Victory.

Notice! When you take your firm stand in the Purity, Beauty, and Perfection of your "Mighty I AM Presence," the whole Power of the Universe rushes to your assistance. When you contact things in the outer world, watch out that you hold control over your feelings. You can love just as greatly in calm poise as in emotional excess or excitement. You do not have to let your human enter in and take you beyond the point of Self-control in your outer activity. By Self-control is how mankind can enter so quickly into the great Victory today.

It is such a great Joy, Precious Ones, to talk to you, to endeavor to help you feel clearly, firmly, definitely your Victory—for It is as sure as Ours if you will only take your firm stand with this. You are coming rapidly to the point where things that you are not aware of, no longer act in your feeling world. Now notice that! Heretofore, many times feeling acted within your world, of which you were not aware until you saw the outer manifestation of it. Very shortly there will be no excuse for that, because the moment a feeling starts you will be aware of what is acting. Please accept this and see how marvelous it is! Then you will not be caught unawares by a feeling projected at you—immoral or destructive activities of any kind which still remain in the charged atmosphere of Earth will not be able to reach you.

Dear Hearts, you have all had these experiences.

I question if there is anyone in the room who has not had this experience: You go into the streetcar and sit down next to someone whose atmosphere is charged with unkind or vicious feeling, and you have to battle that repellent radiation. Most of the time you do not pay attention to it, but it begins to act in your feeling world. Then after it gains a momentum, you cannot get control of yourself because of the outer accumulated pressure which rides in. If the first moment such a condition begins to act in your world, you seize it and stop it, it does not gain a momentum.

The same way with appearances: If you would instantly say to any discordant or limiting appearance, "Oh no, you have no power!" you would stop the whole activity and keep it from entering into your world to affect you. As you gain a momentum, you will find such things will give you one look and go in the other direction. You have no idea, Precious Ones, how these limiting destructive forces, in the control of this energy, know their Master. Just the minute they see you know what is acting, they will cease to bother you. I tell you these old discordant things hold sway only because previously you have not understood how to be alert. These feelings begin to act and revolve in your feeling world before you actually know what is occurring. Then many times people have a battle on. It would not be a battle at all if they really knew, in the Knowledge of the

"Presence," how to charge the mind and body, how to call the Energy to sweep out all discord—then replace it with the Ascended Masters' Substance and Self-dominion.

Precious Ones, My Joy is boundless in having this opportunity to convey My Feeling and My Words into your world. When I say "My Strength," I mean the Strength of My "Mighty I AM Presence" to assist you with Its Knowledge and Strength, until you hold your own Scepter of Dominion in your hand so firmly that no longer can anything disturb or bother you.

I leave with you the Great Love, Light, and Blessing of Bob, Pearl, Rex, the Great Host of Ascended Masters, and the Great Master whose Name is not yet given to the outer world—the Teacher, the Instructor in the use of the Great Light Rays in the Retreat in Arabia. He said to Us recently in certain Instruction He was giving: "My Children, when I had looked upon the failure of mankind through so many centuries, I could hardly have believed that so much was possible for the Children of Earth as has been accomplished in two years."

So Beloved Ones, you can see as these Great Ones do who have gone through so many centuries observing mankind's inability to attain their Freedom; then when you see humanity's great Inner Ability coming forth into action, it is very wonderful indeed. The Infinite Light and Blessings of your "Mighty

I AM Presence," the Great Host of Ascended Masters, and the Fullness of Their Active Presence and Power within you, take full Command of your mind, body, world, your Heart, and especially your feeling world! Release such a Mighty Radiance that you clearly and definitely feel your Certain Victory—NOW! Will you not accept It and be free?

Our Love enfolds you forever in Its Transcendent Light and Strength to your Complete Victory. I thank you!

OUR BELOVED PEARL'S
DISCOURSE

RATANA'S HOLLYWOOD GROUP — HOLLYWOOD, CALIFORNIA

APRIL 6, 1937

THE Victory of the ages is here, Beloved Students of the Light, with no uncertainty! The Glory of the Light expanding from the beloved Students of the "I AM" throughout America is beautiful, transcendent, and the most encouraging thing which mankind could witness.

It has been Our Privilege since the Dictations began before your recent Class, to go to various parts of America and observe that which was going on from the entire activity among the Students of the Light throughout your country. It has been most gratifying, most encouraging, and even the Divine Director said, "It is beautiful to behold!" So you may know when a Great Being of His Authority speaks those Words of Encouragement, it is far more than My Words convey to you.

For your encouragement and strength, I wish to say that Saint Germain came to Me in our great need in San Francisco, where I lived with an aunt and where Bob and I had been very happy. Then Bob went forth, and I thought I was left quite alone. One day, Saint Germain came, when My Heart was reaching out so earnestly for love and happiness, because My dear old precious aunt did not know how to give out love and kindness. She did what she thought was right; but you who have so great a Love poured out to you and are people who release so great a love yourselves, can hardly imagine the condition that existed just at that time.

However, in My great Call to God, one night I suddenly awakened. I was just a little girl, and there My room was filled with a soft Golden Light. In the concentrated part of the Light, I saw this Radiant Presence and lo, It was Saint Germain. The curious thing about it was, I was not frightened. I just felt within Me that it was the Answer to My Call, and surely it was.

Then He said: "Child, you shall grieve no more, and you shall have the outpouring of the love that your Heart craves, from the most unexpected Source. You are not to speak of My visit to you to any living person! This will be a secret between just us. I will train you, instruct you in Laws, the Understanding of Laws that you do not imagine as yet exist. As you gain in this Understanding, you will find your being filled with love and happiness, and then a great sense of freedom. I will come at regular intervals and teach you."

Just at that time I was not attending the public

schools, and He said, "Now do not be disturbed about that," for I wanted so much to go to school. He explained, "I will take care of all that." Then He would send — I wonder if you will quite understand this, yet I feel I must tell you. The Messengers have told you how the Ascended Masters may project a Form of Themselves. When Saint Germain could not be present Himself, He projected this Form of Himself, through which He taught Me many, many wonderful things.

Then one day He came Himself, after Bob had become associated with Mr. Rayborn. With that peculiar twinkle in His Eye, He said, "Don't you think you should go and visit your brother?" I said, "I should love to very much, but I have not the means to go." "Well," He said, "I think We can take care of that." So I awakened one morning a short time after and there on My table was money to defray My expenses. In the exuberance of My Joy, I was about to rush forward and tell My aunt, when all of a sudden I stopped right in the floor. Then I remembered that our contract was one of secrecy. So I stopped to consider. Then I knew, through My feelings, I was not to let her know.

So I went forth to visit Bob, as I thought, and to My utter amazement found others who knew Saint Germain. Can you feel the happiness which filled My being through that Experience? Words could not convey it. Then came the great revelation that Nada's mother had been trained by Him, during all the years He had been training Me. I found She had made the Ascension. The day came when it seemed to Me My Joy had reached its limit. I went with Rex, Nada, and this Good Brother to Table Mountain. I felt impelled to go away a short distance by Myself, and there before Me was this Great Majestic Being, the God Tabor.

As He talked to Me, I realized—just through a mighty flash of feeling—that We were all being directed by a Mighty Intelligence clothed in a Dazzling Form of Light. I want to tell you, Precious Ones, that Cyclopea, Arcturus, the God Meru, the God Tabor, and the God Himalaya are Beings who, the first time one sees Them, seem almost terrifying in Their Majesty, Their Beauty, the Intensity of Their Light, and the Perfection which They are—yet with all that Great and Wondrous Power, as gentle as a mother with her child whom she loves more than anything in the World. When it is necessary, like a flash of lightning Their Limitless Power can be released, which is to perform a given Service.

Tonight I will try to convey to you, into your feelings, the enormous Service which They render mankind constantly and have throughout the centuries, although mankind until now has known almost nothing at all about It.

We love you, Precious Ones, to whom Saint Germain

has brought so much, and whom We love more than any words could ever tell in the World. Yet, We must love Our own "Mighty I AM Presence" first. You know that is rather a difficult thing sometimes, when One has done so much for you. Only if you were in My position at the time He came to Me and began My training, could you possibly know what My feeling is tonight as I endeavor to describe briefly something of My Experience.

I found in the Rayborn home those kindred ones already prepared. Yet He had not permitted Me to say a word to Bob. Then I sent forth a Mighty Call to Saint Germain and I said, "Oh, isn't it possible for Bob to have this Understanding, so We can go forth together?" That which occurred shortly afterwards proved My Call was answered. Precious Ones, as in these Experiences which were Ours, do you not see that every one of your Calls must be answered also?

It cannot fail, if you will follow what He tells you —give your love and adoration to your "Presence" first! Then if at any time you feel a little inability so far as your outer requirements are concerned, call to some One of the Ascended Masters. They will always answer. It is the Law of Their Being and the Law of yours that every Call for Light, Freedom, and Understanding must be answered! If you are not aware of it immediately, please do not have a feeling that your Call has not been answered. It always is! That is why tonight, and every day during the past twenty or more days, there has been pouring into your feeling world the Glory of Those who have been in your midst.

Try to feel, as I am sure you are more and more each day, the Great Reality of these Great Ascended Beings. They are so Real! One day you shall know it; but until you do, will you not feel that Our Experience is Real, and that We bring It to you for your strength and encouragement; that you may feel closer, closer, and closer to Us, until all human doubts and questionings are forever dissolved and disappear from your world?

May I ask you to silence that human viciousness wherever you go and meet vain intellects which try to criticize these Books or that which goes forth in the Magazine because they are written in simple language? That is all done for a purpose, so mankind may not be confused by involved terminology in any of the expressions used. The Ascended Masters could quite readily use such technical terminology that you could not understand a word of it, but that is not the purpose of this Work.

The purpose of this Light of the "Mighty I AM Presence," as the Tall Master from Venus said in the beginning, is that It must come forth in simple language which mankind can understand, and be free from the confusion of oriental or technical terminology. Will you spread this Great Truth everywhere?

People having vain intellects try to complain. Think of it! Who in the world of human activity is authority? The human mind has concocted all kinds of things for itself and has created the most outlandish words for scientific explanation, when a word of four or five letters would have carried its meaning much more efficiently. Wordiness and involved terminology is vanity of the intellect! Those precious ones do not know that; but such accumulated activity which has become dominant within them causes them to feel that in order to maintain authority, they must use so-called technical terminology.

Think of it, Precious Ones, those Great Beings, who have such Infinite Wisdom, always use simple language which even a child can understand! This is the need of humanity today, because the world—through the old occult methods of former schools, metaphysics of every description, religion, and science—has tried to clothe the Infinite, Wondrous, Beautiful Truth with technical terminology, and it has but clouded the understanding of mankind. You today are fortunate enough to have come within the Radiance of Saint Germain and the simple Teaching which He has given forth. Yet It is so Majestic and All-powerful in Its Action that It should silence every intellect which would try to find fault with It. So, if you will, you may render a great service by putting this before the people who complain that they think it should be in a more scientific language.

You see, Precious Ones, Those who really know are like a child in Their gentleness to mankind; for the Great Master Jesus said with such Authority, "Except as ye become as little children, ye cannot enter the Kingdom." Do you know just what that means to you today? It is just this. It means in humbleness, in kindness, gentleness, and gratitude is your Doorway into the Kingdom of Heaven, which is the "Mighty I AM." It fills the Earth with Its Happiness, Beauty, and Perfection, which is not found in the creations of mankind. All who enter into this Great Truth know quickly that the greatest happiness which they have ever known through human achievement or human contact, was but a fragment in comparison to the great flood of Joy and Happiness which comes from an Ascended Being or from your "Presence," and We found that too.

When Beloved Bob was brought by Saint Germain to the Cave of Symbols and His first experience began, it was the most beautiful thing, Precious Ones, that anyone ever witnessed. The eagerness, the joy, yet without impatience, with which He entered into the Instruction Saint Germain offered — and His speed of Attainment has exceeded anything any of Us has accomplished, because of His great joyous acceptance of everything which Saint Germain asked Him to do.

So it is with you today. Just maintain the great

humbleness in the human, kindliness, gentleness, and yet firmness when it is necessary in meeting human creations. You must not forget that. When you are meeting destructive forces, you must be dynamic and firm! Otherwise it will sweep you under! It is a dominating force; but when you understand your "Presence" and then are firm in refusing to give power to appearances of any kind, then in Its Great Calmness you release from your "Presence," at your Call, abundance of all you require to govern you and your world and give you the Infinite Protection of your "Presence."

We have endeavored to convey to you the Truth from various angles, and show you that you do have Real Dominion; for you have Invincible Protection in the Tube of Light about you from your "Presence." It is only when you give power and attention to something outside of your "Presence" or listen to foolish gossip, that you open — shall we call it — a tiny crack in the door of your world. If that is kept up, the door is pushed open more and more, until finally there comes a great rush of destructive force into your world, and an accident, an operation, or something of that kind occurs.

Precious Ones, oh, that you might understand tonight your Great "Presence" in Its Fullness, and that discord in the feeling is the cause of everything which besets your human form — either disease so-called or that which requires, as mankind thinks today, something to be removed from your body to give you freedom. Because of the belief of mankind, it does sometimes seem to be necessary; but when you think of it in comparison with your "Presence," well it is not really necessary, is it? When you know your "Presence" enough, Precious Ones, you will never need any outside assistance of any kind. Neither will you require the surgeon's knife to remove some part of you which seems to be obstructing the way.

Oh, it is so wonderful! Yet do not misunderstand Me. For those of mankind who know not this Great Truth, assistance is required of nearly all which the doctors or surgeons can give—except serums.

Today in the great Expansion of this Light, Beloved Ones, you are the most fortunate of beings, for I repeat to you again: the Expansion of the Light within your Heart and your world is the infinite, positive proof of your achievement during these many months since the Messengers have come to you. Do you think you love them? So do We! Remember how Nada, Rex, Bob, Mr. Rayborn, and Myself love them. Can you imagine Our Gratitude for this Blessed One's coming into Our midst and opening the Door for Saint Germain to come and render the Service He did for Us? Can you? You do feel, I know you do, how greatly We love him and his precious ones. How we long to pick up these two blessed ones, Don and Marjory, and carry them away with Us. There are others of the young folks for whom We would love to do that too. If they will give the full power of their attention in joyous, harmonious determination to the Great Source of Life, their "Mighty I AM Presence," who knows how quickly that might be.

Oh, We would so love to just take away from you — instantly — everything within your feeling or mental world which longer deprives you of the Great Perfection which your "Presence" is and holds for you. It is everything! There is not anything else! These things in the outer world to which you have given such power, and thought were so necessary, are sometimes but a barrier to your Great Freedom.

Not that everything in the outer world which is of use should not be all beautiful and wonderful; but it is according to the way you qualify it, is it not? You see, your qualification is operating all the time. If you requalify the Energy from the "Presence" with something which harms you, then you are at fault, are you not? This is why We keep bringing you back again, again, and again to these simple Fundamentals which, once you grasp them, will send you forth like a rocket into your Complete Freedom.

With Ourselves and the condition which the Great Law provided, We were so quickly freed from, not only the contact, but the disturbances of the outer world. Then with Saint Germain, We saw how the great, great Harmony in Our home had meant so much to Our progress. Our home was Our world, Precious Ones! Your home is just your world! It is not a building in which you may be dwelling, but your home is really your world! When you have come to acknowledge your "Presence," you have entered into your Real Home. As you steadily and surely give attention to your "Presence," It purifies, beautifies, and perfects your home, which is your feeling world. Then outer manifestation of every description must come into the Harmony which is within your feeling world. Do you not see that no great harm could come into your world if your own feeling world were cleansed and purified?

Beloved Ones, whenever you call the Power of the "Presence" forth into action, be sure that you have harmonized yourself first! Call on the Law of Forgiveness for any mistakes, and place yourself in the proper position for the Energy from your "Presence" to come forth untouched by your power of qualification, to render you the Perfect Service for which you are asking. Do you not see, Beloved Ones, that if you call your "Presence" forth with dynamic energy today for a given purpose, and tomorrow you become violently angry or critical of a person, place, condition, or thing, the energy which you have already called forth is compelled to take on the quality with which you charged it? I cannot see how anyone can fail to understand this simple Law. Anyone can, with the Determination of his "Mighty I AM Presence," allow the "Presence" to hold Its Dominion in his world, through himself.

Tonight as the Blessed Ones are pouring forth Their Mighty Radiance to you, join Me, oh, Beloved Ones, in the full acceptance of Their Eternal Freedom and All-powerful Activity within you, your world, and your activity. As you do that, you have no idea how powerfully It will act. You are the decreer of your world. You are either receptive or repulsive to the Perfection of this Great Energy. If you are discordant, you are repulsive; if you are harmonious, you are receptive to the Great Powers of your "Presence." Then Its Powers go forth unchallenged, unqualified, and carry Its Perfection into your world where nothing unlike Itself can possibly exist.

You know the old saying that two Hearts beat as one? Tonight, there are many Hearts beating as one. We are all beating as one Heart in this room. Oh, Precious Ones, it is the most magnificent thing on the face of the Earth to find those so loyal to the Light, whose attention is so wonderful that it beats as one Heart—the Heart of the "Mighty I AM Presence"; the Heart of Divine Order and Perfection. Oh, I rejoice with you so tremendously, as do the Others present, that you have become able to still yourselves enough to allow this Great Work to be done—this Great

Assistance to be given to you.

Many times We four Children just burst into a Song of Praise for the Light which is coming into humanity. We look at Our Blessed Saint Germain sometimes almost in awe at the Majesty and Power of His Achievement for mankind. Then He turns and looks at Us and, with that curious twinkle in the Eye, says, "Children, stop that nonsense!" It is very wonderful to enter into such Happiness which is Ours. You can, no question about it! Remember, We are standing by until your Achievement, until your Victory, provided you do not chase Us off.

Oh, We know so well what mankind goes through in the experience of human creation. Today We stand wholly free from it and the two worlds meet—the human and the Divine. May I ask you again tonight, how many of you precious, earnest Students have thought where and what that dividing line is? The Messenger, I think, has intimated it to you several times.

Do you know that dividing line is your Higher Mental Body? There is where the human ceases and you become Free. Feel, just for a few moments, the full Power of your "Presence" acting through your Higher Mental Body. It knows your every requirement. Then just feel—decree—*silence* while I assist you, that now your complete Victory and Freedom is forever sustained—remembering always that your determination is the outer activity of the Inner Will of the "Mighty I AM Presence."

Then your determination becomes the dominant Power of your "Presence" to fill your world with Its Perfection. So as you accept this into your feeling world, We decree that it goes into Action Invincible to produce those results for you. Now remember, the Life, the Intelligence which enables you to accept this fully is from your "Presence." Do you not see, as you come to more fully understand it, that all activity is from your "Presence"? If left in Its Complete Freedom, It would produce quickly the full Perfection which It is.

Now call your "Presence" to take full command! Refuse, Precious Ones, any longer to allow any outer appearance to make you feel discordant! Refuse to listen to any discordant gossip of any kind—because that is the thing, if you listen to it, which in a moment finds entrance in your world and begins to whirl and disturb you. This is why the Messengers and We keep pouring into you this Mighty Truth of the Law which, if entered into, will produce your freedom from destruction.

Of course, We never feel disappointed. Yet We want so much to give Assistance—for instance, for someone's voice or for their health. But if that one allows the human to rush in or cause him to feel a lack of energy and strength, well, We just try to redouble the

Radiance so as to dissolve the acceptance of the appearance of lack, energy, strength, or help. What you can do, Precious Ones, is to stand firm, and with determination refuse acceptance of anything you do not want.

Now remember, Beloved Ones, in all these Dictations that are given to you, We are talking Heart to Heart. We are not talking for the criticism of some college professor. We are talking in simple language, that your Heart may feel this Sincerity, this Loyalty, this Truth. This is how you receive the greatest Power and Assistance which is possible to be given in the Great Stream of Energy from your "Presence."

When you sit down around your table at dinner in the evening, do you stop to realize whether you are discussing things you speak of, in collegiate, technical terms or not? Do not think this sounds critical; but in some of the schools We have visited, there was not any real help being taught. You know We had a very wonderful school. Now, We have a still more wonderful one! Some of the schools in which there is such great dignity and such great assurance that every word must be just so, the blessed students most of the time are being deprived of the freedom which is theirs. They are not gaining the feeling of what their instruction should convey. Think! The feeling is the important thing; for unless the feeling is improved by the language, it has become a dead language, so to speak.

This is why I am giving you this explanation tonight; for those who have been unfortunate enough to criticize the Expressions of the Ascended Masters will do very well not to do it again. We are not concerned about the intellectual opinions of Our Language, but We are putting this Truth forth in Words that carry Our Feeling of your Victory and Freedom into your world. Is that not the most important thing which mankind requires today?

Even in Our Experience in the Retreat in Arabia, We have been given such marvelous use of the Light Rays in Their various Colors and Their Mighty Activities. Already, We have been able to use Them in an amazing manner for the Blessing of mankind and the Earth. Oh, how We have been able to stop destructive activities by these Rays — We little children! We call Ourselves "little children" yet.

Do you not see, Precious Ones, how there is nothing in the world that can limit you? Even this Good Brother's Experiences on the side of Mount Shasta, in the assistance of the Ascension, is positive proof. Anyone who disbelieves it is foolish indeed; but there stands the Living Proof to all mankind, if they can accept it. Mankind is not limited today in a single thing that individuals do, except through their own human concepts, through their feeling world.

As this Good Brother has told you many times, he had no idea what was to be done. Yet a Mighty

Service was rendered through his Higher Mental Body, the "Mighty I AM Presence." Now that Blessed One has returned to serve him as long as he wishes to serve humanity in the outer form. No earnest effort is ever lost. Your motive within you is the determining factor in your Life. If your motive is wrong, it will bring unhappiness and failure. If it is pure and good, it will lift you to the Height of Eternal Freedom. Then go forth in the Glory of your "Mighty I AM Presence," and have the Freedom which It brings.

Our Love in Its Eternal Purity and Perfection enfolds each one of you like a Mighty Garment of Light. With your permission, We shall qualify It to be Eternally Sustained and Active within and about you, to produce much more quickly your Freedom and Perfection from all limitations of your own creations or otherwise — that you may quickly enter into the full conviction of your "Mighty I AM Presence," to be the Governing Factor, the Governing Intelligence of your world.

Stop forever giving power to appearances and conditions which are less than the Perfection of the "Presence"! Do not feed your Life energy into appearances to harm and limit you. Do not! I plead with you, Beloved Ones! It is only through your attention that you feed your Life energy to limit, disturb, and cause you to fail. So take your stand, if you have not already, in the great Firmness of your "Presence"! Refuse any longer to give any person, place, condition, or thing which is destructive any power whatsoever — any acceptance or power! Those limitations came of your own creation and they have no power, except what your Life has fed into them.

Therefore, understand this simple Explanation, oh, Children of the Light! Go forth from tonight in your Mighty Victory, free from the substance which has been qualified by human creation. Go forth, I say, in the Power of your "Mighty I AM Presence" — the Glorious Victor, the Glorious Commanding Presence over all human things. The Assistance of the Great Divine Director, before whom Universes bow, has been offered and given you. Should you ask for any greater Assistance in all the World of God's Creation than that? It is offered to you as a glad free Gift of Love — from His Heart to your Heart — through the Power of Divine Love and Its Eternal, Mighty Sustaining Power.

We love, We bless, We thank and praise you into your immediate Victory, into your full, complete Consciousness of your Freedom and the Power of the "Presence" to stand guard over you. Call the Violet Consuming Flame into action to prevent anything coming forth of your human creation from ever causing you accident or disturbance of any kind. Keep calling your "Presence" forth to rush Its Mighty Violet Consuming Flame from your feet up. At night when you sleep, call the "Presence" to pass It through the mattress of your bed, and keep this Sustained Activity going through you. Then see and feel the peace and rest into which you will enter.

I love you, I love you, I love you, oh, Precious Ones, Beloved Children of the Light! I love you, We all love you—forever!

FINIS